Mary Lee

July 22, 1987

The Ear Is Human

James J. Kilpatrick
Illustrations by Charles Barsotti

The
Ear Is Human

A Handbook of
Homophones and Other Confusions

Andrews, McMeel & Parker
A Universal Press Syndicate Company
Kansas City • New York

Library of Congress Cataloging-in-Publication Data

Kilpatrick, James Jackson, 1920-
    The ear is human.

    Includes index.
    1. English language—Homonyms—Dictionaries. 2. English language—Usage—Dictionaries.
I. Title.
PE1595.K47   1985   423'.1   85-15816
ISBN 0-8362-1258-4 (paperback)
ISBN 0-8362-1259-2 (hardbound)

Contents

Contents

Contents

Contents

Preface

The English language, that marvelous instrument of communication, has a lamentable way of yielding sour notes. Our mother tongue is filled with look-alikes and sound-alikes, and these cause incessant trouble.

Homonyms are not much of a problem. A homonym is defined as "one of two or more words spelled and pronounced alike but different in meaning." For example, a *sally* is both a sudden activity and a witty remark. In a recipe, we find a pinch of salt; on a ship we find an old salt; in the laboratory we find deposited salt; of an industrious youth we say that he has earned his salt. A post is part of a fence; it is the morning mail; it is a military assignment; it is a bugle call. As a verb, *to post* has to do with sending letters, riding horses, publishing notices, and entering figures in a ledger. But because homonyms are spelled alike, while occasionally they may trip up a reader, they rarely unhorse a writer.

Homophones are the truly mischievous tricksters. Webster's defines a homophone as "one of two or more words pronounced alike but different in meaning or derivation or spelling." That definition is too narrow for my purposes in this little handbook. The homophones that cause the greatest embarrassment are words that are more or less alike in their pronunciation but are quite different in both meaning and spelling. Those redheaded troublemakers, *effect* and *affect*, are homophones.

The only thing a writer can do with homophones is to master the little critters by memorizing their variant spellings and meanings. Mnemonic devices are not much help. Computer programmers have invented marvelous pieces of software, capable of pointing a cursor at every misspelled word in a piece of copy, but these are no help either. The software that recognizes *waive* also recognizes *wave*, and it finds both words correctly spelled. How is a poor word processor to know that hay is not bailed, but rather baled?

Other languages, to be sure, exhibit the same opportunities for a pratfall. In French, *tante* is an aunt; *tente* is a pavilion. When something in France is green, it is *vert*; but we also run into *verre* (glass), *vers* (verse), and *vers* (toward). French writers stumble over *foi* (faith), *foie* (liver), and *fois* (time). Readers who are multilingual doubtless could think of similar examples in Spanish, Italian, Portuguese, and for all I know, in Oriental tongues as well.

The purpose of this book is mainly to have fun with words. A secondary purpose is to provide a handy lexicon of homophones and other confusions, complete with Horrid Examples, in the hope of assisting writers who may have an uneasy sense that something in their prose is Not Quite Right. Such writers could always consult the nearest dictionary, of course, but in that event they would miss the drawings of Charles Barsotti.

My collection, as you will see, is highly selective and deliberately limited. In her *Dictionary of Homonyms* (Amereon House, Mattituck, N.Y., 1981), Louise Ellyson racked up about 4,000 entries, including several hundred homophones and almost 500 trickers she termed "bruisers." Most of these are so rarely mixed up that it seemed pointless to include them here. Not many writers, we may fairly assume, are likely to confuse *bastard* and *bustard*, or *beer* and *bier*. Neither have I fulminated at great length on the confusion of *who's* and *whose*. The writer who cannot get straight on *there* and *their* is beyond my instruction.

With regret, as beyond the scope of this opus, I also have tossed out several citations of the wild confusion that results when communication collapses between the listening ear and the typing finger. There was the Florida editor who wondered why churches get involved in politics "in the face of all the calamity it earns them." There was the New Jersey columnist who "mustard up my courage" to go sky-diving. In Amarillo, an editorial writer said earnestly that "of all the courts in the state, the Texas Supreme Court should be above approach." In Louisiana, newspaper readers saw a photo of flood victims "clamoring out of their undulated car." In Baltimore, a feature writer explained that a popular TV show in the Soviet Union "came into being as an anecdote to the stodgy way Moscow was presenting foreign news."

As writers, alas, we do tend to lose our concentration. A reporter for United Press International in Alabama regretted the inaccessibility of Gov. George Wallace, "but maybe reporters are at fault because they have not banned together." In Indiana, an editorial writer quoted the Preamble to the Constitution; one purpose of our charter, he recalled, is "to secure the blessings of liberty to ourselves and our prosperity." A young woman was admitted to the previously all-male Southwest State Technical College in Alabama; a reporter noted that at first the men "were less than thrilled when the bespeckled redhead appeared in class." A retired rear admiral at the Center for Defense Information had praise for a famous colleague: "Admiral Rickover worked deciduously during his 54 years of naval service." In Portland, the Oregonian quoted legislator Wayne Fawbush. Once a member winds up on Ways and Means, he said, "even the most ribald conservative is forced to confront responsibility."

These things are addictive. In Baltimore the Loyola Federal Savings & Loan advertised for a chief operating officer: "exceptional benefits and prerequisites." In South Carolina, during the presidential campaign of 1984, a man-in-the-street explained why he was opposed to the Democrats' vice-presidential nominee. "I shutter to think about Mrs. Ferraro sitting next to the button," he said. In Trenton, a sportswriter rued the declining fortunes of the New York Mets: "The shame is that they are not going down with the consummate grace of a Rommel or a Montcalm, but instead in a fuselage of cheap shots . . ." In Florence, S.C., the Huggins Sheet Metal Company advertised its services; it installs "heat pumps and duck work." In Roanoke, an editor boasted fondly that his wife "is a passed master at cornbread baking." In Portland, Ore., a columnist recalled with pleasure Mayor Daley's exultation at Kennedy's victory in 1960: "Together we must rise to higher and higher platitudes."

Readers of my syndicated column have sent me a hundred such

glorious bloopers. A reporter for the AP interviewed Louisiana's Gov. Edwin Edwards and asked if the governor would cooperate with the U.S. attorney in a certain investigation. "I called him," quoted the AP, "and told him that I was at his beckoned call." In the same mind-wandering vein, a reporter in Indiana quoted the manager of construction at a new school: "The new roof is on, and for all intensive purposes the project is done."

"That was John McEnroe," said a TV commentator, "exchanging epitaphs with the spectators." In a Sunday supplement in North Carolina, a writer told us about restored railway yards near Salisbury. "After lying decadent for several years, the railroad nerve center is alive again." In Paola, Kan., the Miami Republican told its readers of a girl who had contacted meningitis. The Palm Beach Post had a story about a woman who was the brunt of numerous jokes. The Richmond (Va.) Times-Dispatch said that by making due with an artificial heart, William Schroeder was showing what real heart is all about.

If I could cite two especially egregious blunders, they would be a matched pair of mangles. In October 1983 UPI sent out a story on the funeral of New York's Cardinal Terence J. Cooke: "As the coffin was lifted and carried to the altar, more than 3,000 mourners sang the hymn, 'O God Our Health and Age Has Passed.'" In Eugene, Ore., the Register-Guard reported plans for the funeral of a much loved minister: A choir "will sing 'There is a Bomb in Gilead.'"

Those are kind of sad. Evidently the mangled passages were a consequence not of inattention but of a misunderstanding in dictation, but even so: It is not unreasonable to expect professional writers to have some minimal acquaintance with two of the most familiar hymns of the Christian church. Many of the other Horrid Examples that follow also are a reflection of sheer ignorance; and that ignorance perhaps is a reflection of the declining esteem in which many of our school systems hold the teaching of English.

I cannot conclude on a melancholy note. Most of my Horrid Examples come from daily newspapers. On behalf of my brothers and sisters of the press, I would beseech your forbearance. It is a minor miracle that a daily paper ever gets out at all. Given the pressure of deadlines, it is certain that mistakes will be made. There may not be time to correct a *breech* for a *breach*. The gratifying thing is that, in relation to the millions of words that pour off the presses every day, so very few errors wind up in print. And it should be said that an erring copy editor may be far more responsible for an apparent blunder than the reporter who wrote the copy in the first place. (I once wrote in a column that investigators "had pored over thousands of pages of relevant material" in the matter of President Reagan's counselor Edwin Meese; in the Knox-ville News-Sentinel it came out, "had poured over," and I was much reproached by Tennessee readers.)

Thus in charity I ask you to assume that the authors of these boners really knew better. That is a doubtful assumption, I grant you, but reporters do get in a hurry, and their minds do wander from the task at hand, and proofreading is like scrimshaw: It is getting to be a lost art. In any event, as Mr. Pope reminded us long ago, to err is human, to forgive, divine.

White Walnut Hill
Woodville, Virginia 22749

June 1985

accede / exceed

The Associated Press put on its wire from Birmingham a story about a judge's ruling in a suit involving an order of an Alabama state official. The plaintiff in the case was a company in the business of disposing of toxic wastes. The judge didn't approve of the order. He said (or the Birmingham News said he said) that the official "acceded his authority."

Nope. The official *exceeded* his authority. He went beyond what was permitted by law. A useful mnemonic device: "Nothing exceeds like excess."

The verb *to accede* is worth a moment. It is one of four verbs that are related by blood or marriage: *accede*, *acquiesce*, *assent*, and *consent*. Each of them means something more than merely to agree.

When we *accede* to something, we do it with reluctance; we are under some pressure; our better judgment may say "no," but all right, "we will accede to your wishes." *Acquiesce* is pretty close; it implies a kind of quiet, forbearing acceptance of a proposition at hand. It carries a faint connotation of giving permission.

Webster's says that *assent* implies an act involving both understanding and judgment, whereas *consent* involves the will and feelings. I will buy that distinction. If the company in the Alabama case had been willing to accept the official's order, the company would have *assented* to it. As for *consent*, it is hard to play with the word without remembering Byron's young maiden, who strove a little while,

and much repented,
And whispering "I will ne'er consent"—consented.

access / assess

A six-column streamer in the Columbus (Ga.) Enquirer provided this doubtful piece of information: "Special Anti-bodies Accurately Access Extent of Lung Cancer." Maybe so, for *to access* has become a verb of art in the arcane new world of computer technology, but as the AP story made clear, the intended verb was *assess*: "Tailor-made anti-bodies can accurately diagnose the spread of a particularly virulent form of lung cancer, researchers say." To *access* something is to get inside it. To *assess* something is to weigh its importance or value.

adieu/ado

In a letter to the Daily Southtown Economist Newspapers of the Chicago area, state Sen. William F. Mahar marked an end to twenty-four years in public life. He had served as a village trustee, as mayor of Homewood, as a state representa-tive, and finally as a state senator. Read the headline over his letter: "Sen. Mahar Bids Ado."

What the gentleman bade was *adieu*. Moral: Do Not Use Foreign Words Unless You Are Certain You Know How to Spell Them.

affect/effect

The Washington Post, in a story about the Federal Trade Commission, reported Chairman Jim Miller's belief that not all markets require policing by the FTC. In many cases consumers are able to spot deception easily on their own "and with relatively little affect on their pocketbooks." What was meant was *effect* on their pocketbooks.

In a flier sent to telephone customers, AT&T spoke of the great divestiture of January 1984. "It effects all of us in some way or another." The breakup of the Bell system actually *affected* all of us. It affected most of us expen-sively and some of us maddeningly.

The UPI covered a survey that found that doctors and pharmacists aren't providing adequate information to drug consumers. "The pharmacist should keep a record of any

allergies and other conditions that may effect drug safety."
The right verb here was *affect*.

To *affect* is to have an influence upon. (It is also to put on
airs, as in "He affected a British accent," but that takes us
off course.) Thus wind *affects* a sailboat's speed. Cheese-
cake *affects* the waistline. Campaign debates may *affect* an
election's outcome, but in 1984 they didn't.

To *effect* is different. It means to bring about or to
accomplish. A doctor's prescription may *effect* a cure. An
act of Congress may *effect* the will of the people. As a
noun, an *effect* is a consequence, or result, or outcome.
The effect of Walter Mondale's good showing in the first
debate of 1984 was to improve his image with the voters;
the effect, as it turned out, didn't last long. Before taking
one more drink for the road, we should consider what
effect it will have on our driving ability.

A note in Webster's Ninth New Collegiate Dictionary
advises us that confusion over the verbs *affect* and *effect*
goes back at least to 1494, so the problem is nothing new.
The point to remember is that when something is *effected*,
it is over and done with; when something is merely
affected, it is only influenced or modified.

affluent/effluent

The Society of Waste Water Engineers held a cocktail party.
It was an effluent affair. Ho-ho-ho. No joke, *effluent* and
affluent sometimes are confused. Both words come from
the same Latin root, with the meaning of *to flow*. When
money flows in, a person may be *affluent*, meaning
wealthy. The noun form is *affluence*. As for *effluent*, in
ordinary usage it's the waste material—especially waste-
water—discharged as a pollutant. If you're into geography
and want to be technical, an *affluent* is a tributary stream;
it flows in. An *effluent* is a branch that takes off from a lake
or river; it flows out.

aid / aide

The State Department put out a statement in 1984 marking the sixteenth anniversary of the Soviet invasion of Czechoslovakia. Then the statement was abruptly withdrawn. It turned out that the text was two years out of date. Reported the Associated Press: "Officials said the 1982 statement was being used as a research aide for this year's anniversary." A two-year-old text might be an *aid* to a writer—a little something helpful to go by—but an *aide* is a person, not a prop.

aisle / isle

In Cape Coral, Fla., a sportswriter for The Daily Breeze went to a boat show and returned with a rapturous report. "As you leisurely stroll up and down the isles," he wrote, "it is easy to imagine . . ." A boat lover might well dream of visiting isles, but what the reporter was strolling were aisles.

Aisle has an interesting etymology. In contemporary usage it means a passage in a church, theater, stadium, or supermarket, but it stems from the Old English word for shoulder and the Latin *axilla*, armpit. It also is traced to the Middle French *aile*, wing. The two roots entwine to produce *axillaries*, the short feathers of a bird. As for *isle*, there's nothing much to be said. Only the professional linguists know why it shouldn't be spelled *ile* or else pronounced *izzle*.

allude / elude

On a Sunday morning in August, according to the Prineville (Ore.) Central Oregonian, "two area drivers were arrested for attempting to allude a police officer." The headline confirmed the story: "Two Nabbed for Alluding."

On a Wednesday morning in March, the Bristol (Va.)

Herald-Courier had the same problem. A prisoner who had been jailed in Knoxville had escaped a week earlier. "He had alluded authorities since."

Two days before the fugitive was alluding near Bristol, the Roanoke (Va.) Times & World-News carried a story about Lefty Driesell, coach of the Maryland basketball team. A sportswriter had said something unkind about the coach, but the coach benignly let it pass. "A younger Driesell might have stomped a foot and protested that he never got any credit from the press for his many victories, eluding to a league dominated by Dean Smith."

Early in 1985 the Portland Oregonian carried a story about Mary Decker's victory in a 2,000-meter run. It was her first win since her famous fall in the Olympics, and she had a special reason to be delighted. " 'This is my first win as Mary Slaney and I'm really happy,' Decker said, eluding to her recent marriage to British weightman Richard Slaney."

One more example comes from The Seattle Times, which carried a straightforward account of Supersonics Coach Lenny Wilkens' appraisal of his team's prospects. Said the coach: "We have no allusions about this year."

Let us get them straight. To *allude* is to make an indirect reference to something. A few weeks after the 1984 election The New Republic, which had warmly supported Walter Mondale and the Democratic Party, turned upon the party platform in a savage editorial. The magazine called the Democrats' idea of a nuclear freeze "a silly gimmick." For The New Republic to say such a thing struck me as "the most unkindest cut of all," and I said so in a column. It was an allusion to Antony's oration at the funeral of Caesar, but it was lost on many of my readers. They rebuked me for a double superlative. Anyhow, I had *alluded* to the play.

To *elude* is to evade or avoid. The verb carries a connotation of adroitness or deception. It is rooted in the Latin verb *to play*. Incidentally, *evade* and *avoid* are not synonymous. All of us have a right to avoid taxes, but it's against the law to evade them. Back to *elude*: There is a noun, *elusion*, dating to 1624, but I cannot recall ever seeing it in print or hearing it in conversation. A magician's disappearing acts are both *elusions* and *illusions*. Ezra Pound's allusions elude me. All clear?

altar / alter

"I want to altar our relationship," said the young man in a note to his young lady.

"Oh, yes, darling!" She replied. "Let us set the date."

Trouble is, the fellow wanted to break their engagement, but alas, he couldn't spell. He had in mind the role of an older brother; she had in mind the role of a wife.

Moral: To *alter* is to change. An *altar* is the table in a church where the rite of matrimony is performed.

amend/emend

Once upon a time in a book I wrote, I referred to Connecticut's Sen. Lowell Weicker as a Democrat, which he ought to be but isn't. Readers called me on the blunder, and in the next edition I restored the senator to the GOP. We had *emended* the text. We had corrected an error. Such emendations are improvements on a written work.

To *amend* also may mean to correct or to improve, but those connotations do not necessarily apply. In a legislative body, an amendment to a bill may add provisions, delete language, or change the meaning altogether.

If you will think of an amendment as a change and an emendation as a correction, you'll have it just about right.

appraise/apprise

During the Ford administration, the White House announced over the Christmas holidays of 1974 that the president intended to nominate a liberal Democrat, Edward Levi, as attorney general. The rumor incensed conservative Republicans and created a messy situation. Columnists Evans and Novak wrote that if Mr. Ford "had been appraised of such determined Senate opposition," he might have dropped Levi before his name surfaced.

In Philadelphia, the Inquirer carried a review of an exhibition of watercolors and etchings by the American artist John Marin. The headline read: "Apprising the Work of True Individualist."

Wrong, wrong! The works of art were *appraised*. Mr. Ford should have been *apprised*. To *appraise* is to form a judgment: Property is appraised for taxation. To *apprise* is more than merely to inform; it implies the communication of something of special interest or importance: Members of the Senate were apprised of the Levi nomination. Sen. Jesse Helms, R.-N.C., was both apprised and surprised, and very much annoyed too.

assay / essay

A book critic, reviewing Philip Howard's *State of the Language*, had a general comment. "The trouble with most books that attempt to essay the state of the mother tongue," he said, is "that they are written by purists intent on proving that we have entered an age of declining standards and linguistic anarchy will soon be upon us." It would have been a better sentence if he had put a period after "anarchy," but never mind. Howard wasn't attempting to *essay* the state of the language, but rather to *assay* it.

The verbs are not synonymous. To *essay* something is to attempt it, often experimentally or for the first time. Thus a novice pianist might boldly essay a program limited to Chopin's preludes and ballades. To *assay* is to analyze or to judge. A miner assays ore; a chemist assays the impurities in water; a critic of English usage assays the state of the language. Those who assay contemporary English and find it moribund are mistaken. The language is in great shape, healthy and virile, and growing all the time.

assure / ensure / insure

The careful writer will feel his way through this thicket. Consider these uses of *insure*.

From The New York Times, in a story about a poll taken during the presidential campaign: "The poll shows, for instance, that voters say, 54 percent to 27 percent, that Republicans are 'better able to insure a strong economy.'"

From the "Dear Abby" column, in response to a letter reminding the columnist that the word "tip" comes from "to insure promptness": "Yes, but in view of the fact, one wonders why the tip is not given in advance so that 'prompt' service would be insured. Because the tip is given afterward, it 'insures' nothing."

From a column by Andrew J. Glass about concerns in the Kremlin: "What concerns the Soviet rulers is the need to reinforce their legitimacy and thus to insure the survival of their system through what looks like tough times ahead."

The lexicographers are not much help on *assure*, *ensure*, and *insure*. Their notes are mostly murk. Let me give the problem a go.

I would reserve *assure* for use in the sense of ending uncertainty or dispelling doubts. Reuters reported from London in January 1985 that Mrs. Thatcher "assured Parliament that she was not proposing that Britain start stockpiling nerve gas; her assurance amounted to a denial of a magazine story."

I would put *ensure* to work as a kind of utility infielder, scooping up everything that is not literally or metaphorically commercial. It seems to me that *ensure* conveys the idea of guaranteeing, or making sure of something, but with no overtones of a contractual relationship. For example, let us give Junior an extra $10 to ensure his getting to the airport on time. Let us understand that no promises will ensure a husband's fidelity. The Washington Post reported a news conference at which John Cowles, Jr., said the family's continued ownership of the Minneapolis Star & Tribune "had been ensured as the result of recent negotiations among Cowles family members."

Finally, I would limit *insure* strictly to commercial propositions only. Let us insure lives and property, and let us be certain we have sufficient insurance against the risks mankind is heir to.

Reverting to the three examples: I would find the Republicans "better able to *ensure* a strong economy." I would go along with Dear Abby, and give the tip in advance "so that 'prompt' service would be *insured*." As for the Soviet rulers, their concern is to reinforce their legitimacy "and thus to *assure* the survival of their system."

Be assured that I claim no infallible judgment on these subtleties. That writers always will disagree on such matters is virtually ensured. No insurance can be written to protect any of us from the risk of a pratfall on this uncertain terrain.

auger / augur

On Long Island, the supervisors of Huntington and Smithtown met to talk about garbage. After a forty-five-minute meeting, Newsday reported, one of the gentlemen said they had established "a personal relationship that augers well."

Editor & Publisher, reporting an address by researcher Ruth Clark, said that she had urged American newspaper editors "to get back to basics." Such a shift in emphasis, said E&P, "augers the beginning" of what Clark said would be "a great period for newspapers."

The word that both wanted was *augurs*, not *augers*. An *auger* is a tool for boring holes. An *augur* is a soothsayer who makes prophecies based upon portents or omens. A motion is in order that *augur* be reserved for highly specialized use in the context of divination, and that both noun and verb be otherwise abandoned. Anyone who would write that something "augurs well" would call legislators solons and say that it behooves the solons to shun the lucre of labor barons.

bail / bale

Comedian Jerry Lewis once told Parade magazine that he grew sick of Hollywood. Everywhere he looked he saw friends hooked on hard drugs. It was like flying in an aircraft with a drunken pilot. "I baled out of the aircraft before it crashed."

The Savannah (Ga.) Morning News carried a colorful account of a shipwreck that swept seven persons into the sea. The survivors managed to board a life raft, where they "set off signal flares, baled water, and shadowboxed to keep warm."

To *bale* is to press a large body of material into a compact mass: a *bale* of cotton, a *bale* of hay, a *bale* of marijuana. The fellows in that life raft would have had a terrible time baling water. They were *bailing* water.

In other meanings, *bail* goes back at least to the fifteenth century, when its most familiar meaning had to do with prisoners. If they could put up *bail* as security for their future appearance, they were released. For whatever it may be worth to know, the hinged bar that holds paper against the platen of a typewriter is known as the *bail*. If you pick up a kettle by its handle (how else?) you are picking it up by its *bail*. And if you want to divide a few head of cattle in a corral, you shunt them into pens. These also are *bails*. We get *bailiff* and *bailiwick* from the same Middle English roots.

baited / bated

In the Tampa Tribune, columnist Ann McDuffie had a lead that must have hooked many readers: "I'm sure you've all been waiting with baited breath," she wrote, "to learn that October is Popcorn Poppin' Month."

In the Indianapolis Star, a reviewer gave generally good marks to the magician David Copperfield. His illusions were enjoyable, but "there really wasn't anything which made one sit on the edge of the seat with baited breath."

In the Omaha World-Herald, a reporter quoted Public Works Director James Suttle on the uncertainties surrounding construction of a downtown overpass. "I know the businessmen are going to be waiting with baited breath."

So far as I know, breath is the only thing that ever is *bated*. Everything else that is closed down or reduced is abated. As for *bait*, one *baits* a hook, a trap, or a recalcitrant witness who is easily provoked. In merry old England, men *baited* bears. Today, in our more civilized time, we bait politicians instead. It's much more humane. But baited breath? Never.

ball/bawl

In Fort Collins, the Coloradoan entertained readers with the story of a bridal couple who sought to be married in a canoe. The bride explained that they wanted to provide a happy occasion, not something sad and mournful. After all, she said, at many weddings "people sit and ball their eyes out." *Bawl*, my dear, *bawl* their eyes out. This is one homophone I positively will not explicate.

bare/bear

In Spokane a sportswriter was looking ahead to the football season. Oregon, he said, "is a team that bares a lot of watching."

An outfit that *bares* is looking for an X rating. The writer intended to say that Oregon *bears* watching. The idiom makes no particular sense, but that is sometimes the way with idioms. Women *bear* children; beams *bear* weight;

people *bear* names; soldiers *bear* arms; and some people can barely bear other people.

barrettes / berets

The AP's man in Yugoslavia filed a color story about a figure skater, Katarina Witt, who was competing in the Sarajevo Olympics. "Wearing a raspberry dress with matching berets in her swept-back hair, Witt is the second East German woman . . ."

Those weren't *berets*, brother. Those were *barrettes*. They were those little ornamental clips that women wear to keep their hair from blowing around. A *beret* is the European version of the Scot's tam-o'-shanter, which is named for the Burns hero of the same name. A *biretta* is that square cap with three ridges worn by Catholic priests. A *Beretta* is James Bond's gun.

base / bass

These homophones are worth a moment not because they're often confused—they aren't—but because they point up an aspect of English that drives foreigners to drink. There is no reason on earth why *bass*, as in *bass clef*, *bass drum*, and one who sings *bass*, should be pronounced to rhyme with *race*, as in horse race. Every other English word that ends in *-ass* rhymes with glass, pass, grass, and so on. When we're talking about the fish, it's bass as in mass. Phonetically speaking, one who sings *bass* with the long *a* is a basso, as in lasso. None of us invented English pronunciation, but all of us can marvel at it.

bazaar / bizarre

Some funny things—bizarre things, you might say—have a way of happening when these two get tangled.

In Eugene, Ore., a local columnist teed off on conductor

A CHRISTMAS BIZARRE

Zubin Mehta. It appeared that Mehta had been in town; the columnist had sought an interview, but had been told the visitor was "too tired" to see the press. "Our disappointment turned to anger when we later learned that while in Eugene, Mehta found enough strength to attend late-night parties, to shop at a Christmas bizarre, and to pitch in a baseball game."

Across the continent, in South Carolina, a reporter for the Beaufort Gazette wrote about a yacht race from Miami to Montego Bay. One of the yachts had run afoul of Cuban authorities and had been briefly sequestered, but things had turned out well: "Despite the bazaar delay, the 'Brigadoon' was the first boat over the finish line."

And in Freeport, Ill., readers of the Journal-Standard may have blinked at an ad for sidewalk enterprises: "Numerous church bake sales & bizarres. Stop in and see."

No doubt about it, a Christmas bizarre and a church bizarre would be worth a reporter's time, and a bazaar

delay would provide abundant time for shopping. The
writers had things backward. The noun *bazaar* dates to the
sixteenth century; its meaning hasn't changed in all this
time: a row of shops or stalls, often used in the United
States for the sale of goods for charitable purposes. The
adjective *bizarre* dates from the mid-seventeenth century;
it carries a connotation of wild eccentricity, striking non-
conformity. Performers of punk rock strike me as bizarre,
but punk rockers may look upon old columnists in the
same way.

bellow / billow

These second cousins may not qualify as true homophones, but they caused trouble for the news editor of the
Eufala (Ala.) Tribune. "Thick clouds of black smoke bel-
lowed high above the burning wooden frame dwelling." He
meant that the smoke *billowed*, a fine sixteenth-century
verb meaning to roll or to surge in waves. The verb *to
bellow* is even older; it has to do with imitating the sound
of a bull. To bellow is to shout loudly; it is to bawl, but I
said I would have nothing to do with bawl.

berth / birth

It was a fine AP photo that ran one day in the Pittsburgh
Post-Gazette. The caption read "Blocked fore and aft by
shipyard cranes, the U.S.S. Connole sits in its birth yesterday."
    That was a *berth* the ship was sitting in. Incidentally,
berth is one of those words, like *cleave*, that can have
opposite meanings. At sea, to give berth is to pass at a safe
distance; ordinarily a helmsman gives wide berth. In a
Pullman car, a berth is never wide; it is narrow. As for
birth, I find nothing of note to remark, except that the
dialectal verb *to birth* dates only from 1906, while *birthday
suit* goes back to 1753. In a New Year's Day piece, colum-

nist Georgie Anne Geyer spoke of 1985 as "still another year birthed by stories of war." Can stories birth a year? I'd give that metaphor a berth—the wide kind.

block / bloc

In political parlance, *bloc* has a well-defined meaning. It is a temporary coalition of often opposing forces who have come together for some particular purpose. In 1981 the Reagan administration was able to rely upon a bloc of Republicans and boll weevil Democrats to win enactment of its tax program. The fact that blocs often are formed to block something provides no reason for confusing the terms. We are free to write of building blocks, heart blocks, pulley blocks, auction blocks, wood blocks, and walking around a couple of blocks, but in politics: *blocs*.

boarder / border

The Bloomington (Ind.) Herald-Telephone covered a murder trial that stemmed from a domestic argument over some stolen cigarettes. "A border at the Bakers' home testified Wednesday that he, not Pedro, stole the cigarettes." A *border* is an edge or a boundary. A *boarder* is someone who regularly eats, and often lodges as well, in an otherwise private residence.

bole / boll

When conservative Southern Democrats got together in the House of Representatives in Reagan's first term, a news correspondent hung upon them the name of *boll weevils*. The defectors had gotten into the heart of the Democratic Party. By voting with the Republicans they were devouring its unity. Many writers, not familiar with cotton, thought the mavericks were *bole weevils*. Not so.

For the record, a *bole* is the trunk of a tree, but boles are not attacked by weevils. *Bolls* are the pods from which the puff of cotton emerges. Boll weevils are terrible things in cotton, but in the House they pulled the Reagan measures through.

borough / burrow

The Portland Oregonian carried an obituary of an eighty-six-year-old biologist whose rewarding career had begun when he began trapping chipmunks and other rodents as a boy. "While at the University of Washington, he discovered that the little known mountain beaver was burroughing in the campus flower beds." The critters were *burrowing*. At one time *boroughs* and *burrows* were spelled identically. A *borough* was a kind of combination fortress and walled town that provided safety from enemies. A burrow was an animal's hole. The city of New York has five boroughs, none of them remarkably safe. In northern Virginia, cattle raisers are plagued by groundhogs whose burrows are dangerous also.

bough / bow

From Ketchikan, Alaska, UPI reported a boating accident. A 24-foot cabin cruiser capsized 300 yards off the Sukoi Islands, but a Coast Guard boat "found passenger Pat McCarty clinging to the bough." Unless some tree limbs were floating around, the gentleman wasn't clinging to a bough but to the bow (the forward part) of the drifting boat. Pronounced identically, the two nouns have the same root in Old English and Scandinavian words for shoulder. The other *bow*—the one that rhymes with *hoe*—is ascribed both to Old High German and to the Sanskrit word for bend.

brake / break

The Massillon (Ohio) Evening Independent carried a dramatic photo of Spanish shipyard workers who were striking in Bilbao. The workers were crouched behind barricades to protect them from "national policemen who were attempting to brake up a demonstration."

In a flier for a home security system, the manufacturer recalled the old days when "we even left the doors open when going next door for a coffee and conversation brake."

Those Spanish police doubtless meant to bring the demonstration to a halt, but they weren't *braking* it up. They were *breaking* it up. As for a conversation *brake*, we can imagine all kinds of statements that might put a stop to further discussion, but that wasn't the intention here. As a noun, *brake* goes back to 1772; as a verb it comes along a century later. A *break* is something you give a curve ball, a dance band, an orthopedic surgeon, or a friend in need.

breach/breech

Only a handful of words rhyme with *each*, but they have a way of giving trouble—*beach/beech*, *leach/leech*, and in the matter at hand, *breach/breech*.

In Winston-Salem, N.C., a columnist for the Journal had fun with a story about police officer Peter Curtis, who was advised at 1:30 a.m. that a naked woman was strolling around the Smugglers Den Campground. It was a "serious breech of the public peace."

Newsday covered a civil trial in which a jury awarded $500,000 to a laborer who had been shot by an off-duty policeman. "We all agreed that the officer's use of excessive force was a breech of fundamental rights," said juror Dennis Reissig.

The Roanoke (Va.) Times & World-News covered a performance of Gilbert and Sullivan's comic opera *Trial by Jury*, and explained that "the plot revolves around a breech-of-promise suit in London, circa 1875."

You don't *breech* rights or promises; you *breach* them. Both words share a common root but they have grown up differently. To speak of a *breach* is to speak of a breaking:

invaders *breach* a wall; a whale *breaches* the surface. To speak of a *breech* is to speak of the rear end or bottom of something: the *breech* of a gun, the *breech* of a pulley block. In a wardrobe, *breeches* (rhymes with witches) used to mean a kind of snug knickers, but lately breeches have come to mean almost any kind of pants that go below the knees.

bread / bred

You wouldn't think this homophone would cause trouble, but it threw a guest columnist for Sun Reporter Newspapers. She spoke of *On Your Toes* as a remarkable addition to the much loved musical theater, "which like jazz is one of a few American-bread contributions to the world of art, music, and dance." I can think of some fine contributions of American bread—the loaves of Pepperidge and Arnold, to mention only two—but most American-bred bread tastes as if it had been compounded of library paste. The word the columnist wanted was *bred*.

breadth / breath

The Wall Street Journal, which usually approaches the flawless level in its proofreading, carried a suspenseful note from the world of banking: "Everyone was holding his breadth to see whether the discount rate would go up."

When we maintain our weight, that's what we all do: We hold our breadth.

bridal / bridle

Reported the society columnist: "Miss Ravenel wore a bridle gown of white satin . . ." No, ma'am. A bridle gown conceivably might be a riding habit, but brides wear bridal gowns. A *bridle* is that ingenious arrangement of bit and reins by which a horse is restrained.

calvary/cavalry

A correspondent for The Associated Press, writing from Crow Agency, Mont., filed a story on the plans of archeologists to begin a dig at Custer Battlefield National Monument. Readers of the Livingston Enterprise learned that the scientists will be searching for the bodies of troopers who never were accounted for "after Custer and his five companies of the 7th Calvary were wiped out by Indians on June 25, 1876." The story went on to explain that "Custer and his calvary were killed to the last man."

There can't be many opportunities these days to write about cavalry, and except at Easter time there's not much mention in the trade press of Calvary. There's no reason to confuse the words, but they constantly are confused. Webster's dates *cavalry* from the mid-sixteenth century, and traces it to French and Italian roots that have given us *cavalier, chivalry,* and *chevalier.* Christians revere Calvary as the hill near Jerusalem where Christ was crucified; by extension, a personal calvary is an intense physical or emotional suffering.

canape/canopy

I am once again indebted to the Livingston Enterprise— more accurately, to one of its advertisers—for an appetizing classified ad:

> FRENCH PROVINCIAL
> TWIN bed with canape and
> box spring. Excellent condition, $150

It is a pleasant vision, is it not? Let us all aspire now and then to cocktails in a French provincial bed. Canapes under the canopy! And if you don't mind, Jeeves, a gin martini on the rocks.

cannon/canon

There is canon law, and then there is cannon law. Ministers
live by the one, artillerymen by the other. When an Episco-
pal priest explained in a church bulletin that cannons
compel the vestry to do certain things, he wasn't talking of
bombardment. He had the word wrong. Canons are the
authoritative regulations of a religious body. An author's
canon is a definitive edition of his works. The two-*n* cannon is what goes bang when the Boston Pops plays the *1812
Overture*.

canvas/canvass

In Seattle, a sportswriter for the Post-Intelligencer
reported that leaders of Washington's largest sports fishing
group "have voted to canvas all of its members to see how
they feel about a proposal to outlaw Indian sales of steel-
head trout." The preferred verb is *canvass*.

Among the Big Three, only Webster's III sanctions both
the one-*s* and the two-*s* spellings for (1) the stuff you make
sails out of and (2) the counting of votes. The dictionaries
of Random House and American Heritage agree that *canvas* is the cloth and *canvass* is the tally. In either spelling,
the word stems from *cannabis*, hemp, known in less botan-
ical circles as Mary Jane or marijuana.

capital/capitol

These trickers have to be mastered by anyone intending to
write of politics or of corporate finance. Alas, at the Harrisburg (Pa.) Patriot News, a couple of staffers hadn't done
their homework.

Under the splendid headline of "Divine Providence," we
learn that "Rhode Island's capitol city is sheer heaven for
those who appreciate architecture, thanks to nearly three
decades of restoration work."

On another day, we read that "Harrisburg may not be known as a fashion capitol, but you certainly don't have to leave the capitol city to find the latest styles."

There may be some mnemonic device—I can't think of a very good one—to remind us that *capital* is the city and *capitol* is the building. Most capitols have domes; domes are round; the *o* in capitol is round. Does that help? Probably not. The other *capital*, the one with the *a*, has to do not only with cities but also with accumulated wealth and with the tops of columns. When Theodore Roosevelt wasn't crying "Bully!" he was crying "Capital!" Good man.

carat/caret/karat

The two that give trouble are *carat* and *karat*. Anyone who has occasion to write about a *caret* presumably knows that a *caret* is that little arrowhead mark that proofreaders use to indicate where matter is to be inserted. So much for *caret*.

A *carat* is a unit of weight, equal to 200 milligrams, that is used only for precious stones. A *karat* is a unit of fineness for gold. One *karat* is equal to $1/24$th part of pure gold in an alloy; thus an 18-karat wedding ring is three-fourths gold and one-fourth good intentions.

If you throw a *carrot* into this linguistic stew, you get a four-way homophone, but it didn't seem necessary to discuss the roots of *carrot*. You can dig them out for yourself.

censor/censure

The words are distant cousins, now far removed from their common ancestor. In early Rome a *censor* was a tax assessor, a census taker, and an inspector of morals and conduct. Through the years the word has come to be used only in the third context. At one time many states had boards of motion picture censors. Maryland's board hung

on practically forever. The only official censors remaining
in American life today are prison censors, who inspect
mail and packages for contraband, and military censors,
who classify documents in the name of national security.
Most cities have unofficial censors who make life miser-
able for librarians, magazine dealers, and the publishers of
textbooks and dictionaries. All this is *censorship*.

Censure is something else. When the Amarillo Daily
News editorialized on the case of Congressman Gerry
Studds, the writer got mixed up. He spoke of Studds' "censorship by his House colleagues," and observed that Congressman Dan Crane "also was censored" at the same
time.

The two men weren't *censored*; they were *censured*. A
censure is an act of more or less official reprimand; it is a
judgment, and a very unpleasant one at that. Apropos of
nothing in particular, it provides a footnote to say that
Studds, who seduced a boy page and thought nothing of it,
was reelected in 1984. Crane, who seduced a girl page and
wept with remorse, went down to defeat.

centenarians/centurions

Kiwanotes, an occasional publication of the Kiwanis Club
of Augusta, Ga., reported that the club had as its guest
speaker Dr. Dexter Burley, a sociologist who specialized in
gerontology. He remarked upon a village in Greece that
reportedly has 433 inhabitants, of whom 29 are more than
one hundred years old. Reported the newsletter: "Most of
these centurions are actively productive, tending their
fields and participating in the leadership of the village."

I'm not certain that anyone other than the editors of
Kiwanotes in Augusta, Ga., ever confused *centurions* and
centenarians, but the image of such aged but sturdy
Greeks is irresistible. For the record, a *centurion* was the
commander of one hundred Roman soldiers; to become a

centurion was a difficult and dangerous task. All that is
required to become a *centenarian* is that one live to be one
hundred years old. More than forty thousand Americans
are centenarians now; in the next century being a centenarian will be no novelty at all.

chord/cord

In the Indianapolis Star, a reporter interviewed a Jewish
spokeswoman on the matter of the Jew-baiting Louis Farrakhan, who had been invited by the Indiana Black Expo to
make a speech. "People can ask whomever they want," she
said, getting the pronoun exactly right. "I just hope that he
will not find a receptive cord among the American people."

Jon-Michael Reed, who writes about soap operas for
United Feature Syndicate, had an item on Shelley Burch.
She was taking a breather from the soaps in order to make a
movie. "Miss Burch is also oiling her vocal chords for
August's National Republican Convention in Dallas."

In Rapid City, S.D., the Journal interviewed an industrious supplier of firewood: "So far this season he's produced 250 chords of wood, using a machine that splits up
to three chords an hour."

From Washington, the Newhouse News Service reported
in January 1985 that former President Nixon was suffering
from shingles. "The announcement struck a cord with the
millions of Americans and their families who have suffered its agony."

The problem with *chord* and *cord* is that we get tangled
in word associations. We associate *chords* with music: It
takes at least three notes, sounded simultaneously, to produce a *chord*. In writing about a singer, we think music,
and automatically a Shelley Burch acquires vocal chords.
No way. Those vibrating things in her throat are vocal
cords.

Now we get into trouble. A cord is a piece of stout string,

right? We have a simile, "straight as a string." We think of a cord stretching from one point directly to another. But do you know what the straight line is that connects two points on a circle? That's a *chord*. My advice is to forget geometry when you're writing about less esoteric *cords* and *chords*.

Chords have to do with music, and by extension with harmony, and harmony pleases. Thus we strike a responsive chord. Perhaps Farrakhan found a receptive chord in Indianapolis.

Cords have to do with—well, cords: umbilical cords, vocal cords, the heavy string with which you tie up a package. As for the busy woodsman in South Dakota, he was turning out cords of wood, each 4x4x8 feet.

Three-way homophones are nothing unusual, but if you're playing word games you can hit for a triple with *cored*.

LAUNDRY SHOOT

chute/shoot

It sounds noisy, and it certainly would be hard on one's shirts, but you might want to check it out from an ad in the Mobile Press-Register:

> NEAR OLD VANITY FAIR
> MILLS off Padgett Switch Rd.
> Brick home in private neighbor-
> hood, screen porch, 3 bedrooms,
> 2 baths, built-in kitchen, unique
> laundry shoot! $60's.

cite/sight/site

The Los Angeles Times Syndicate sent out a sales promotion letter, inviting editors to consider the columns of Art Buchwald. Among other things, Buchwald "has just been sited by the National Braille Institute as the most read columnist—or feature—by blind readers nationally."

In Miami, a sportswriter for the Herald noted that John McEnroe had decided not to enter the new Lipton International Players Championships. "He has sited a number of reasons why he won't play . . ."

The Coastal Journal of Bath, Maine, announced a concert at which flutist Bonita Boyd would appear. Ms. Boyd, said the paper, "has been sighted as one of today's major talents."

Parade magazine carried a feature story on riverine warfare in Vietnam. "It was a relief," said the author, "to have the river banks defoliated so the ambush sights were further back, and not at point-blank range."

A flotilla of tall ships visited Rochester, N.Y., in the summer of 1984. The Democrat and Chronicle provided a neat list of twenty-six "parking sights" that would be available to persons coming to the Genesee River by car.

The Wall Street Journal, reporting on the New

Hampshire primaries of 1984, let us know that "Sen. Gary Hart has set his sites on Mr. Mondale."

Let us clean up the dishes. Columnist Buchwald and flutist Boyd weren't sited; they were *cited*. Those weren't ambush sights and parking sights; they were *sites*. The verb *cite* carries two meanings, one commendable, the other authoritative. We can cite a soldier for bravery, or cite a columnist for wit, or cite a flutist for her technique. A lawyer cites precedents by way of authority for the position he is taking.

A *site* is a place. That is all a *site* is: the site of the battle, the site of the proposed convention center, the site where John F. Kennedy was shot.

A *sight* is everything else. A spectacular show is a sight to see. A person who has been gardening in mud is a sight. A hunter looks down the sights of his rifle. A navigator determines his position by taking a sight. Bankers know all about sight drafts. We set our sights on achieving a particular goal. And will we give up? Not by a damn sight.

clew / clue

Let us suppose that Miss Marple, Agatha Christie's delightful detective, announces in despair that "I haven't a clew." What is the dear lady saying?

She is more likely talking of sewing than of detecting, though the point is debatable. A *clew* is a ball of thread or yarn. In the American Heritage Dictionary, that is about all a clew is. (Well, a clew also is one of the lower corners of a square sail, but that's getting a bit arcane.) In Webster's, a *clew* is both a skein of thread and also a piece of evidence that leads one to the solution of a problem. Webster's sniffily lists clue as no more than a variant spelling of *clew*.

American Heritage is the better authority on this one. In either spelling, the word stems from a root meaning *thread*. American Heritage cites the ingenuity of Theseus in using a clew—a ball of thread—to guide him through the

Cretan labyrinth. The preferred usage is *clues* for detection, *clews* for needlework.

coffered/coiffured

The Miami Herald provided readers of its real estate section with an informative essay on concrete construction. Poured concrete walls are unusual today, but in the 1920s and 1930s many builders employed the technique. They also used concrete cast in various sculptural forms. "For instance, coiffured ceilings formed by a reverse molding process as the concrete was poured can't be duplicated with today's concrete block and dry-wall building materials."

A coiffured concrete ceiling would doubtless be a permanent adornment, though getting it in place could mean some hairy moments. The desired word was *coffered*. A coffer in this sense is a recessed panel. In a more familiar application, *coffers* is the pejorative word used by editorial writers when they want to belabor a point: the coffers of the Chamber of Commerce, or the coffers of organized labor. A cofferdam, for the record, is the watertight enclosure that builders pump water out of in order to get piers or foundations in place.

collaborate/corroborate

The Canton (Ohio) Repository came up with a feature story on the Mary Worth comic strip. The strip evolved from Apple Mary, which had been created by Martha Orr Hassle, but in the mid-thirties Mrs. Hassle wanted out of her contract. A father and son team picked it up. "The elder Saunders, who had corroborated on a comic strip that evolved into the still popular Steve Roper, got his shot at Mary."

One who *corroborates* a statement confirms it. A defendant's testimony is corroborated by the testimony of other witnesses. The elder Saunders hadn't corroborated; he had *collaborated*, which is to work jointly with others on a particular effort—usually an intellectual effort. The word also contains an ugly meaning: In wartime a *collaborator* is one who willingly assists the enemy.

commensurate/commiserate

A classified ad—a sort of sad classified ad—appeared in The Seattle Times:

> ARTIST
> MAJOR northwest silkscreen
> Co. is looking for an artist with
> a strong background in graphics
> & cartooning. Portfolio req'd.
> Salary commiserate w/abilities.

Perhaps the prospective salary was something to evoke

commiseration—the penniless artist is a familiar figure—but the company wasn't really appealing for sympathy. The wanted word was *commensurate*, which means corresponding to.

complementary / complimentary

A guest columnist in The Washington Post fired a salvo at the Post's anti-Reagan business editor, Hobart Rowen. "Instead of the administration's monetary and fiscal policies being contradictory, as Rowen asserts, they were quite complimentary."

Nope. The policies were *complementary*. The policies weren't drawing praise (certainly not from Rowen); they were mutually supplying and complementing each other.

Compliments are nothing but flattering remarks—the kind of remarks that will get you everywhere. *Complements* are lots of things. The complement of a ship is the whole crew, officers and men alike. You find complements in geometry and other areas of mathematics. In music, a complement is the interval it takes to complete an octave. And in a sentence such as "He thinks Rowen misguided," the word *misguided* is a complement. It certainly wouldn't be intended as a compliment.

confirmation / conformation

A staff writer for the Asbury Park Press undertook to explain the rules of the Eatontown Dog Show, but the sentence he formed in his mind wasn't the sentence that came out in print: "The more than 1,600 pedigrees who turned out for the event were judged in one of two categories, confirmation, how the dog looks and moves, and obedience."

The judges may have looked to one another for *confirmation* of their judgment, but it was *conformation* they were seeking in the pedigreed mutts. As exhibitors in horse and dog shows will tell you, conformation is akin to beauty, which lies in the eye of the beholder. Perfect conformation means that all an animal's parts are in exactly the right proportionate dimensions, but judges can get pretty opinionated about what proportionate dimensions are perfect. Obedience presents no such opportunity for subjective judgment. The mutt heels or he doesn't heel. End of discussion.

convocation/invocation

A vanishing Southern custom is the prayer before a sports event begins. The custom attracted the eye of a sportswriter for the Spokane Spokesman-Review who was in Knoxville covering the 1984 football game between the University of Tennessee and Washington State. "Just prior to tonight's kickoff in Neyland Stadium, a man of the cloth will deliver the convocation to as many as 91,000 believers. What they believe in is the UT football program . . ."

Knoxville's man of the cloth—a seventeenth-century expression still in wide use—was about to deliver an *invocation*, asking the Lord to watch over the players for both teams but perhaps to watch over Tennessee with an especially kindly eye. An invocation comes first; the benediction comes last. A *convocation* is the assemblage that one prays over. Episcopalians have more convocations than anybody.

council/counsel

The thing to learn on this one is that for everyday purposes, *council* is a noun only. It is an assembly with some sort of governing or deliberative purpose—a city council, a council of elders. The troublemaking homophone *counsel* is both a noun and a verb. It always has to do with advising or consulting—legal counsel, public relations counsel, the counseling of a faculty adviser. A city council could employ counsel, and the counsel after a time would counsel council. No problem.

dairy/diary

Under a photo of two upstanding gentlemen, the Anderson (S.C.) Independent-Mail had an embarrassing cutline:

> *Diary Breeder Award*—Veteran County dairyman Jack Dobbins, right, was presented the S.C. Purebred Diary Cattle Association's master breeder award at the 1984 S.C. Diary Conference at Clemson University. Making the presentation is Harold Longshore, the association's vice president.

The author of that caption lost his struggle with *dairy/ diary* by a score of 3-1. It may help to remember that my *diary* (with the long *I*) is something that I write. A diary breeder would be a publisher and promoter of personal journals. A dairy breeder is someone who raises cows for milk production.

dam/damn

It was hard to tell what the Texas dog owner was mad about, but his ad in the Amarillo Globe sounded doggoned exasperated:

> BLUE and fawn Dobermans.
> AKC championship bloodlines.
> Priced to sell. I own sire and damn.
> See to appreciate.

It's not hard to deduce how *dam* got to mean the female parent of an animal; in this sense the word obviously comes from the same root that leads eventually to "There

Ain't Nothing Like a Dame" in *South Pacific*. Since the fifteenth century a *dam* also has been a structure for impounding water.

Our most familiar and perhaps the mildest of forbidden four-letter words has a longer history. Webster's dates *damn*, which came to English straight from the Latin, to the thirteenth century. By Shakespeare's time, around the turn of the sixteenth century, the word had become a familiar intensifier: "Where is that damned villain Tranio?" and "Out, damned spot!" The noun, in the sense of "I don't give a damn," dates from 1619.

In Parade magazine, a reader inquired if it is true that neither Queen Elizabeth II nor Danielle Mitterrand "gives a tinker's damn about clothes." The Morrises, William and Mary, offer us two theories on the old phrase. One school holds that tinkers were low fellows, given to such excessive swearing that a *tinker's damn* was worthless. Other etymologists believe the phrase dates from the period when a tinker, repairing a hole in a pot, would press a small pellet of bread against the hole while solder was applied. When the solder set, the pellet—the *tinker's dam*—was discarded. You pays your money and you takes your choice.

deceased / diseased

In March 1985 the publication Stamp Collector reported the discovery of one more copy of a stamp known to philatelists as "the Glasgow Error." The stamp was issued by the U.K. in 1964 to mark the fiftieth anniversary of the Battle of the Falkland Islands in World War I. Somehow the denominations got mixed up and a "6" appeared where "2 $1/2$" should have been printed.

"Less than 20 copies of the error are known," said the editor, writing *less* when he should have written *fewer*. "The latest one was discovered by a Boston collector while helping to settle the estate of a diseased friend."

The friend, we may reasonably assume, was not sick; the friend was dead. The friend was *deceased*, a soft seventeenth-century adjective drawn from the Latin for *to depart*. The word carries a faint whiff of formaldehyde; it is a word of last resort, to be used when all else fails.

deferential/differential

The Mobile (Ala.) Press-Register interviewed the young TV anchorwoman who charged that she was fired in part because the news director thought she was "not differential to men." Christine Craft, meet Ron and Jane Cease, husband and wife members of the Oregon state Legislature. The Associated Press in Salem did an interview. "Even though the Senate is considered the 'upper chamber,' he said that as a House member he wasn't overly differential to the state senator who happens to be his wife."

The wandering word in this instance was *deferential*, meaning attentive or respectful. The adjective has sugar in it; it suggests a touch of sycophancy, a kind of obsequious servility. I have looked up *differential* in three dictionaries. What's a differential? Beats me. Look it up yourself.

defuse/diffuse

The American Bar Association, concerned about a popular image of lawyers as high-priced fee-grabbers, published an article of advice to members of the bar. Attorneys should respond quickly to inaccurate statements about attorneys' fees or earnings. "This will diffuse rumors before they begin."

In the Wichita Eagle-Beacon, a columnist recounted an incident in a restaurant. His dinner companion lit a cigarette, and at once a woman in the next booth cringed in distaste. "But before she had a chance to orate, my friend,

seeing her displeasure, immediately put out her cigarette
. . . The situation was immediately diffused."

The Denver Post, in a feature story on Kentucky's Gov.
Martha Layne Collins, noted that in her campaign "she
dealt directly with the issue of her sex, at the same time
diffusing any negatives."

Whoa, there! Nobody wanted to diffuse anything. The
ABA's whole idea was not to diffuse but to defuse the
rumors about high fees. To *diffuse* is to spread out, scatter,
transmit freely. The lost word was *defuse*, which is what
one does to potentially explosive situations.

deluding / diluting

Over the objections of Councilman Vernon Winter, the
Rock Island, Ill., City Council voted to contribute $7,500
toward the Quad Cities Open Golf Tournament. Mayor
James Davis said the money would come from the city's
"pillow tax" on motel and hotel accommodations, but
Winter was not convinced. "We're diluting ourselves," he
told the local Argus, "in believing the QCO brings in
tourism revenue from outside the area."

Diluting? Perhaps the councilmen were spreading themselves a bit thin, but if the dissenting member was right,
they were really *deluding* themselves. It's easy to do if golf
is your game.

demur / demure

A correspondent for Writer's Digest interviewed author
Peter Straub not long after Straub and a collaborator got an
astronomical advance on a horror novel. "Although he
demures from discussing actual figures, Straub admits
that 'the advance was one of the biggest ever paid.'"

A Southern newspaper (not otherwise identified)
reported in a story from U.S. District Court that an
attorney had demured to a suit for damages. This was a

woman attorney. For a moment it appeared that this Georgia Portia had given the judge a coy glance, but that wasn't it at all. She had *demurred*; she had filed a demurrer, a pleading that says, in effect, that even if everything you say is true you still don't have a case. Southern girls are famous for being demure; they also are fond of having good times. It is from these characteristics that a Southern axiom emerged: demure, de merrier.

deserts / desserts

The Sarasota Herald-Tribune once devoted an enthusiastic editorial to prison reforms in Washington state. "The new state law," said the Herald-Trib, "is based on the principle of just desserts: You do the crime, and you pay the price."

So attractive a principle prompts a thought that cherries jubilee might be the just *desserts* of an arsonist. The word the writer wanted was *deserts*, and the word is a tricker. Pronounced DES-ert, it means an arid, barren land. The Gobi and Sahara are DES-erts. Pronounced des-ERTS, it means a deserved punishment. The two-*s* des-SERT causes no such problems. It's the pie, ice cream, or whatever, served at the end of a meal.

die / dye

In the summer of 1984, an estimated eighteen hundred bicycle enthusiasts pedaled the 192 miles from Seattle to Portland. Dan Healy, of Kent, Wash., told the Portland Oregonian that he had a great time. The paper reported: "The tool and dye maker did, however, take a spill."

It's a good bet that the biker who took the tumble wasn't a *dye* maker; he was a *die* maker. To make a dye, you take a pigmented material, turn it into a solution, *et voila!* We make the pink pants blue. Thus *dye* is the word we want if we feel compelled to write that someone is a dyed-in-the-wool Republican.

A *die* is something else entirely. A die is a mold into which molten metal is poured. A die also is a tool for stamping an impression into some object or material. At the gambling table, a die is one of two or more dice.

disassemble/dissemble

In Birmingham, Ala., a basketball team from Kentucky soundly defeated a team from Brigham Young. The Augusta (Ga.) Chronicle gave the story a sizable headline: " 'Cats Dissemble Cougars 93-68."

Ah, no. To *dissemble* is to put on a false appearance, and evidently there was nothing phony about the Kentuckians. The wanted word was *disassemble*, to take apart. A 25-point margin of victory has the ring of a convincing disassembly.

disburse/disperse

In Stuart, Fla., the prospective purchasers of a four-acre tract of land on Jupiter Island fell into a dispute with the owners, but not before the buyers had given the real estate brokers a $25,000 deposit. The Stuart News reported that the brokers "deposited the money into an escrow account, agreeing to disperse the funds in accordance with the conditions of the sales contract."

In Rochester, N.Y., a machine tool plant fell upon hard times and had to close its doors. The Democrat and Chronicle explained that a $4,475,000 loan from Lincoln First Bank "was fully dispersed to the company last September."

Even the Encyclopedia Britannica can err on this one. In its entry under the heading of "riot," the Brit informed us that England provides harsher penalties than the United States "when rioters refuse to disburse after they have been ordered to do so."

Crowds are *dispersed*. Money is *disbursed*. The easy way

to keep straight on this one is to remember that disbursing is what a bursar does. *Disburse* also provides a fine rhyme for *purse*, which is what money is paid out of.

discreet/discrete

Henry Kissinger, the bon vivant and former secretary of state, is one of a very few persons high in public life who have mastered the writing art. His memoirs put him in a class with such stylists as Disraeli and Churchill. Consider this paragraph:

"No charge recurs more frequently in our political debate than the cliché that a problem should be resolved by diplomacy rather than by power. But the idea that power and diplomacy are separable and discreet falsifies the essence of each. Power without purpose leads to posturing; diplomacy without power exhausts itself in rhetoric."

You can be certain that the Hon. Henry was not speaking of the notion that power and diplomacy are "separate and discreet," though that is the way it came out in the Miami Herald. His word was *discrete*, which describes entities that are individually distinct and unconnected. From the same root we derive *discretion*, which involves not merely the quality of being discreet but also the capability of making choices. Diplomats, who must be discreet, seldom have opportunities to deal with matters that are wholly discrete; in foreign affairs, as Kissinger used to tell us, almost everything is connected in some way to almost everything else. Kissinger himself was indiscreet on only one known occasion. That was when a microphone he thought was off in fact was on. Otherwise, as he would tell you, his record for discretion is wholly without flaw.

disillusion/dissolution

In Canton, Ohio, a Common Pleas jury awarded a woman $28,000 in damages against an attorney who had repre-

sented her in a divorce case. Her lawyer in the suit for damages said the lawyer in the suit for divorce had charged the plaintiff $1,450. The Canton Repository provided a helpful explanation: "As part of the disillusion, she paid her husband $5,000."

Sad to say, in the realm of marital affairs, dissolution almost always is a product of disillusion. At the end of this litigation the plaintiff must have retained few illusions about both her former husband and her former lawyer, but at least she had the $28,000.

divers / diverse

The best advice here is to forget you ever saw *divers*. It is an uptown word meaning various, several, or sundry. If your purpose is to write of things that are various, several, or sundry, in heaven's name, why not use *various, several,* or *sundry*? If you write of "divers possibilities," people will think you're talking of something going on at the swimming pool.

While you're putting *divers* back in the bric-a-brac box, you might as well put *diverse* in with it. All it means is *different*. Everybody knows what is meant by *different*, but *diverse* could throw a few readers into puzzlement. They might guess that "diverse possibilities" were alternative rhyme schemes.

dribble/drivel

In the summer of 1984 I wrote a column about a bill, then pending in Congress, that would have adversely affected cooperatives organized under the Rural Electrification Act. I was all for the bill. In the Fort Collins Coloradoan, the general manager of the Poudre Valley REA gave me a hiding. He was dead set against the bill. In a letter to the editor, he said that Kilpatrick's comments were typical statements of those well-meaning, misguided, ill-informed, self-appointed saviors of the federal budget. "The heart of his dribble centered around two points . . ."

Reading these reproaches, I was reminded of a story told on columnist Art Buchwald. He once poked fun at Eisenhower's humorless press secretary, Jim Hagerty, and Hagerty blew up. He publicly denounced Buchwald for writing "unadulterated rot." Buchwald drew himself to his full height and called it a lie. "I write only adulterated rot," he said.

Well, it isn't *dribble* that I write. No, indeed. I write *drivel*. Sticks and stones may break my bones, but those who mean to hurt my feelings with words had better get straight on the words.

dual/duel

To write that someone had a *duel personality* would evoke images of pistols at dawn. Let us not confuse *duel* with

A DUEL PERSONALITY

dual, as in dual carburetors, dual pianos, and a dual-laned highway.

eclectic / electric

Eclectic is one of those out-of-town words, like causal, that practically invite typographical error. A Washington correspondent for The Wall Street Journal covered confirmation hearings for Martha Seger, a nominee to the Federal Reserve Board. During the hearings, said the Journal, "Miss Seger described her monetary policy views as electric. 'I'm a garbage collector,' she told the committee."

The word deserves better treatment. An *eclectic* person is the discriminating sort, one who picks the best of this and the best of that, and draws upon various sources to put together a philosophy, or a literary style, or a system of bidding in bridge.

eek / eke

The Tropic supplement, which runs in the Miami Herald, carried an interview with an escapee from East Germany.

The young man got in trouble for being too closely involved with a peace movement. "His protests meant he had been barred from a university education and he had eeked out a living, selling books or television sets, while dreaming of emigrating to West Germany."

In Chicago, Criminal Court Judge Robert L. Sklodowski told the Sun-Times he was shocked by the release of a criminal he had sentenced some time before. "This was a vicious, outrageous murder of an old man who was only trying to eek out a living."

As an ejaculation of surprise, *eek* does very well, though its contemporary use appears to be largely confined to comic strips in which women see mice. The wanted word was *eke*, which means to get something the hard way. It can be used without the *out*—The survivors eked their way from the swamp—but it looks funny that way.

elicit/illicit

Cosmopolitan magazine once kindled our libidinous imaginations in a piece about hypnosis: "Memories illicited under hypnosis tend to be mixed with fantasy."

The Oak Ridger, of Oak Ridge, Tenn., reviewed a movie whose plot turned on a town's discovery of a rich lode of coal: "This illicits greed in many of the town's residents."

In Motor Trend magazine, a writer appraised the aerodynamic skirts, the chin spoiler, and the unusual wheels of a new model Saab. "The effect they have on the familiar Saab shape is too dramatic not to illicit a strong opinion one way or the other."

From a Sunday paper identified only as the "Herald-Times" comes a feature story about American Coaster Enthusiasts, an organization of twelve hundred members whose obsession is to ride roller coasters. At Kings Island near Cincinnati, the Coasters got a thrill from "The Cobra." Said the reporter:

"The mere thought of riding standing up, coupled with

the immediate 95-foot drop into a 360-degree vertical loop followed by a 560-degree horizontal loop that puts riders parallel to the ground, illicits the best of screeches from male and female alike."

Dear, dear! A Cobra with a 560-degree horizontal loop surely would terrify riders (and it doubtless would terrify navigators also), but the more serious problem is with *illicits*. The twists of The Cobra cannot illicit screeches, nor can the shape of the Saab illicit opinions. A discovery cannot illicit greed, and hypnosis cannot illicit memories, even illicit ones, for there is no such verb as illicit. What the several writers wanted was *elicit*.

To elicit is to draw something out, often with a connotation of reluctance or opposition: On cross-examination, the district attorney elicited an admission that the defendant . . . Something *illicit* is something unlawful, but the adjective implies a certain clandestine or surreptitious character. We would not speak of getting a ticket for illicit parking or of being indicted for filing an illicit tax return. The word has the softness of slippers on dark and secret stairs. Someone whispers of a couple: They are having an illicit affair.

elusive/illusive

"The homeless people of South Florida are an illusive group," reported a writer for The Miami Herald, "visible yet unknown and uncounted."

Well, maybe, but the orphan word that should have been given a home in that sentence was *elusive*. To be *illusive* is to be deceptive; a magician's tricks are illusions. To be *elusive* is to be hard to catch.

entomology/etymology

Under a dateline of Athens, Ga., UPI reported upon the spread of bee mite infestations in several states. An effective insecticide is available in Europe, but it has not yet been approved for use in the U.S. UPI was quoting Dr. Alfred Dietz, "professor of etymology" at the University of Georgia.

It seems unlikely. Dr. Dietz, we may surmise, is a professor of *entomology*. The word stems directly from the Greek *entomon*, insect. Its confusing sound-almost-alike, *etymology*, also has Greek roots. It is the study of words or other linguistic forms by tracing the history of their origins and usage.

For keeping straight on these matters, *-Ologies & -Isms*, a thematic dictionary produced under the chief editorship of Laurence Urdang, is a useful handbook. Among the "ologies" that writers should know about are *macrology*, an excessive wordiness; *psilology*, a love of vacuous or trivial talk; *lexicology*, the writing of dictionaries; and *semasiology*, the science of semantics that deals especially with changes in the meanings of words. People who love to argue about these things are *logomachists*. Join the club!

exercise / exorcise

In the first game of the 1984 National League playoffs, the Chicago Cubs routed the San Diego Padres 13-0. It was one of the most lopsided victories in playoff history, and after their years of enduring the pangs of defeat, the Cubs were ecstatic. In the Clearwater (Fla.) Sun, a Knight-Ridder correspondent launched into his story: "It was as if the Chicago Cubs were in a hurry to exercise the 39-year-old ghosts that haunt the friendly confines of Wrigley Field."

It would have been interesting to have a photo of those 39-year-old ghosts exercising—doing calisthenics, perhaps, or jogging around the outfield with their vapors flapping.

The wanted word was *exorcise*. It means to expel something menacing or oppressive, usually by incantation or ritual. In the case of the hapless Cubs, none of their rites—including five home runs on that glorious day—sufficed to exorcise the ghosts. The spooks followed the team to San Diego and hexed the Cubbies there.

exhume/exude

Many writers, even professionals with long experience in the field, suffer now and then from the ailment known as heterophemism. Urdang defines it as "the unconscious tendency to use words other than those intended." A copy editor at the Pensacola News Journal may have been suffering from such a spasm when he wrote the head over a story about a pitcher for the Atlanta Braves. This optimist was certain he could pitch the Braves back into contention in the National League. Said the headline: "Perez Exhumes Confidence After Mid-Season Outing."

The Braves' confidence may have been moribund in the summer of 1984, but it wasn't so dead that it could have been *exhumed*. That is what you do with corpses that have been buried. The verb is rooted in the Latin *ex* (out of) plus *humus* (earth). It's a fair guess that the editor meant to say that Pascual Perez was *exuding* confidence, but the editor's mind wandered out of the base paths and past a graveyard.

expatriate/ex-patriot

A correspondent for the Chicago Tribune interviewed track star Zola Budd on her arrival from England for her ill-fated run in the Los Angeles Olympics. The "South African ex-patriot" was too shy to talk directly into a microphone.

In the Seattle Times, a list of the evening's movies on TV featured a classic film on Channel 2—*Casablanca*, in which Humphrey Bogart plays the role of "an ex-patriot American casino owner in French Morocco."

At the Indianapolis Star, a book editor took a look at the latest compendium from the Paris Review. "Ever since the Paris Review was founded in 1953 by George Plimpton and other young American ex-patriots searching for the ghosts of Hemingway and Fitzgerald . . ."

Conceivably an *ex-patriot* (one who formerly was a patriot but cannot be termed a patriot now) could also be an *expatriate* (one who has left his own country to live elsewhere), but the combination would be unusual. In *Casablanca*, Rick was a nice guy, but patriotism was not his gig.

faint / feign / feint

Only God and a few absent-minded writers know what these words have in common, but the words do tend to get confused.

In the Sun News of Myrtle Beach, S.C., the drama critic let us know about a coming production of the Grand Strand Players. They were doing a new play, laid in a hospital. The playwright had gathered material over the preceding two years "by feinting illness as a patient" at several South Carolina institutions.

In The Washington Post, a movie reviewer explained the plot of *My Favorite Year*, starring Peter O'Toole as the bibulous Alan Swann and Mark Linn-Baker as the neophyte writer Benjy Stone. At one point "Benjy feints when his mentor Swann urges him to rappel off a skyscraper."

Taking them one at a time: To *faint* is temporarily to lose consciousness, to pass out, to keel over. To *feint* is to pretend to attack at one point in order to conceal a real attack at another point. As for *feign*, it's a nice thirteenth-century word meaning to pretend, to dissemble, to imagine. If that South Carolina playwright had faked a faint, he would have been feigning, not feinting.

fair / fare

You wouldn't think The New York Times would foul up on *fair*, but it has. In a story from Paris on parliamentary elections in Europe, we were informed that "Under the circumstances, several parties representing the strongest symbolic rejection of the governments in power faired well, leaving Europe with an appearance of fractiousness and division."

In Mobile, the Press-Register let us know about rush-hour traffic on a Thursday afternoon in May. "Rush-hour traffic did not fair too well."

The Eufala (Ala.) Tribune managed to err in a 60-point headline: "Eufala City Schools Fair Well in Meet." The Tribune had company in the Amarillo Daily News: "Local Students Fair Better on SATs than State Average."

Lackaday! There is a verb, to *fair*, but that verb is the special province of joiners and cabinet makers; it involves fitting pieces together so that their external surfaces go smoothly together. In ordinary parlance the verb we want is *fare*. We fare well in our endeavors, or we fare poorly. If we bid fairwell to a friend, we're hoping he finds a good water supply.

faze/phase

In a north Texas paper, a feature writer told the story of a sixty-eight-year-old woman, blind for many years, who sought a corneal transplant. Her ophthalmologist told her there was only one chance in a hundred that the operation would restore her sight, but "even this doctor's discouragement didn't phase her."

In Asbury Park, the Press did some man-in-the-street interviews following the first debate between Ronald Reagan and Walter Mondale. Said one of the men in the street: "I listened to both of them and they haven't phased me one way or the other."

In the comic strip "For Better or for Worse," wife warns husband that their children intend to dress as rock stars. "Heck," he says, "it doesn't phase me one bit."

So far as I know, the verb *to faze* is used only in negative constructions. It means to be disconcerted, daunted, or taken aback. I cannot recall ever hearing anyone admit to being affirmatively fazed; it's always the patient who was *not* fazed, or the voter who was *not* fazed. The homophonic verb *to phase* ordinarily comes hand in hand with a preposition; we phase in, phase down, and phase out. We take things in phases, step by step. Almost any process can be phased, but only people are subject to fazing.

feat / feet / fete

In Vancouver, Wash., the Columbian carried a feature story about a crackerjack typist, Betty Lee Baird, who can type as many as 166 words a minute—"a fete that earned her the title of National Typing Ambassador in 1980." Remarked the contributor who sent me the clipping: "She must have been typing the party line."

In the summer of 1984, actor George Stanford Brown (from *Mod Squad*) appeared in a drama that dealt with a great American hero who cheated on his income taxes. Commented Newsday: "Talk about your feat of clay!"

During the Los Angeles Olympics, the Greeley (Colo.) Tribune managed to stumble in a headline: "America's Carl Lewis Wins Again, Matches Owens Fete in 1936."

It's a fair assumption that everyone knows what *feet* are. They are the appendages we walk with; there are three of them in a yard; they are what humans and animals stand

on. When metal type is off its feet, the type is not squarely fixed in its chase. To be at a woman's feet is to be under her spell. So much for *feet*.

A *feat* is a special kind of deed—an act performed with exceptional strength, stamina, skill, boldness, or courage. The word goes back to fourteenth-century England.

A *fete*, imported from the French, is a lavish or elaborate party, often staged *al fresco* (you know Al, the Italian bartender), usually featuring costumes or entertainers. You can pronounce it to rhyme with *bait* or *bet* as you please, but both Webster's and American Heritage prefer the long *a*. A *fait accompli* provides a homophone to go with *fete* and *fate*. As a general rule for a general readership, it's a good idea to shun foreign phrases, but there's no good English substitute for *fait accompli*.

flare / flair

The Washington Post provided a profile of Ed Zschau, the high-tech entrepreneur from California who won election to Congress in 1982. Said the Post: "His political flare first emerged in his role as director, and later chairman, of the American Electronics Association."

The Eufala (Ala.) Tribune covered an altercation that began at a pool table and led to a death. "Witnesses at the scene told police that the two exchanged words outside the establishment, tempers flaired, and a fist fight was the result."

My favorite logomachist, J. T. Harding of New Jersey, is a veritable hound after flares. He has cited the orchestra conductor, presiding over the *1812 Overture*, who "conducted with great flare," presumably with a torch.

A *flare* in any form, whether of light or emotion, as a noun or a verb, is something temporary or sudden. A *flair* is a noun only; it comes from the French word for "sense of smell," but over the centuries, it has come to mean an instinctive ability or talent to do a particular thing. The

infant Mozart had a flair for the harpsichord. The fashions
of M. Dior have a flair all their own. A "political flare"
would be a hot argument on the hustings.

flaunt/flout

In Washington, D.C., residents of the congested Adams-
Morgan neighborhood appealed to the Police Department
for help. The problem, reported The Washington Post, is
that the residents "are plagued with motorists, particularly commuters, who flaunt parking regulations."

Another problem of law enforcement in Washington
drew the attention of the old Washington Star: "Since the
no-smoking laws have gone into effect, there have been
widespread reports of smokers openly flaunting them."

One more news story out of Washington, this one by The
Associated Press, dealt with the government's inability to
enforce a law designed to halt the flow of illegally earned
dollars into foreign accounts. In the Portland Oregonian
the story drew a four-column headline: "Foreign Tax
Havens Flourish, Flaunt Law."

In each instance, the wanted word was *flout*. To flaunt is
to wave something, to brandish or to display it, ordinarily
in an ostentatious or contemptuous way. The winner of a
civil suit might emerge from court *flaunting* his decree. To
flout is to beat, to violate, to treat with scornful disregard.
Scofflaws do not flaunt the parking regulations, they flout
them.

flea/flee

Readers of the Cambridge (Md.) Daily Banner picked up an
interesting bit of information about a flood in Missouri.
The flood, said the Banner, caused residents "to flea their
homes."

A fleaed home, on top of a flooded home, would have
been one affliction too many. The wanted word was *flee*, a

fine old twelfth-century verb, meaning to run from danger or from an unbearable situation.

formally / formerly

The trustees of Indian River Community College in Florida approved several changes in staff at the college's FM station. Reported the Stuart News: "Wendy Tedding, formally development specialist, has been assigned to handle public affairs and special features."

Virginia's Sixth Congressional District, which had been held by the Republicans, fell to Democrat James Olin in 1982. The Roanoke Times & World-News editorialized on the GOP's prospects for regaining the seat in 1984. Ray Garland, a strong contender, had announced his candidacy. Willis Anderson, who only recently had become a Republican, was another possibility. "He hasn't formerly announced for the nomination, and may not now that Garland is in the race."

In Portland, a medical corporation opened a new facility for the treatment of minor injuries, illnesses, and routine medical problems. Reported the Oregonian: "The care center will be housed in a three-story building which formally was occupied by Tarbell Realty . . ."

Interesting images, these: a starchy development specialist, a real estate salesman in tuxedo, and a politician who hadn't "formerly announced." There's no need to explicate *formally* and *formerly*. The words aren't confused out of ignorance; they're confused out of inattention.

forward / foreword

You would think that people who write about books would know the difference between *forward* and *foreword*, but it is astonishing how often the two words are confused.

In The New York Times, a reporter covered an exhibition at the Metropolitan Museum of Art. " 'Here, for the first time, is seen the continuum of Portugal's experience of porcelain,' writes Philippe de Montebello, in his forward to the show's handsome 89-page catalogue."

In The Washington Post, we learned that biographer Kit Denton had run into much difficulty in obtaining records of the court martial of Breaker Morant. "In the forward of his first book, he blamed the British government for refusing to release the records to him."

In the Manhattan (Kan.) Mercury, a reviewer discussed the first edition of William F. Buckley's *Up from Liberalism*. He recalled that "John Dos Passos wrote the forward to this book twenty-five years ago."

Those little preliminary essays are *forewords*, for Pete's sake; they are words that come *before* the book itself. To be sure, an appealing foreword is intended to entice the reader into going forward, but they're entirely different words.

foul/fowl

A columnist in the Borger (Texas) News-Herald provided a fine reminiscence for Thanksgiving Day on the time his

A FOWL BLOW

stepfather dispatched him and his cousin Billy to bring in a chicken from their backyard. "He did such a job of telling us which foul to gather up that he forgot something—he didn't say to bring dinner back dead or alive." The boys captured a hen and brought her to the kitchen. "The foul flew across the kitchen, letting everyone within hearing distance know she wanted no part of this Thanksgiving business."

An AP correspondent in Michigan had things punfully straight when he wrote about a truck accident on Interstate 94. The truck "took a foul turn and dumped thousands of chickens across the road . . . State and local police joined residents in rounding up the liberated fowls." When the AP story got to the San Antonio News, an absent-minded headline writer erred: "Foul Flee Crash Scene."

In the Miami Herald, a staff writer put together a backgrounder on the Sikhs of India and explained why they have experienced millennial problems: "The Sikhs were neither fish nor foul since they were neither Hindus or Moslems . . ."

The author of that last sentence had all kinds of problems: He went for a cliché; he got the cliché wrong; and the second time around, he forgot that *neither* takes *nor*. As an adjective, *foul* means putrid, rotten, grossly offensive; applied to the weather, it means stormy; in sports we find the foul blow in boxing and the foul ball in baseball. A *fowl* is a bird, and for everyday purposes the word applies to adult domesticated chickens, turkeys, ducks, and geese. If the reference is to game birds, the reference should be to *wildfowl* or to *waterfowl*. These are homophones to watch with care. If anyone ever called the legendary Frank Perdue a foul breeder, Perdue would punch him in the nose. It takes a tough man . . .

gait / gate

In the Cumberland (Md.) Times/News, a medical columnist addressed a concern about flat feet among athletes.
Not to worry, said the columnist.Many superb athletes
have flat feet. "You might be interested," he added, "in
watching some of the best athletes in various team sports
and notice how odd their gates and feet directions are."

Both *gait* and *gate* spring from the same roots in Middle
English, but an athlete's gate would be something like a
stage door—an entrance for players but not for spectators
and reporters. Webster's gives as the first definition of *gait*
a manner of walking or moving "on foot," but the much
more familiar usage deals with the movements of horses
and dogs.

gall / gaul

The wine columnist of The Seattle Times interviewed
Orville T. Magoon, a California winemaker whose label
features a picture of the famed British actress Lillie Lang-
try. Magoon said he almost took her picture off his bottles
at one time, but "I'm in love with Lillie and I just
couldn't." Said the Times: "It gauls him that Lillie is
mostly remembered for her infamous affair with Edward,
Prince of Wales."

The word is *gall*. As a verb, it means to irritate or to vex,
with a connotation of long-suffering resentment. The
nuance here is of a continuing pattern of insolence or
annoyance. In an equine application, a horse is galled
when a loose or ill-fitting saddle rubs a sore on the horse's
back.

As for *gaul*, the only Gaul most of us will ever know is
Caesar's capitalized Gaul, the one divided into three parts.

genteel/gentile

There were some red faces at an advertising agency when the ad appeared in Southern Living magazine for a hotel in Charleston, S.C. "Travelers discovering the Francis Marion Hotel find elegant rooms and a gentile Southern atmosphere."

Not funny. Not funny to Jews, anyhow. Any hotel or restaurant that provided only a *gentile* atmosphere would be in trouble with the feds who enforce the Civil Rights Act of 1964. What was intended was *genteel*, a nice, soft, old-fashioned word that conveys the idea of upper middle-class elegance. Something genteel is something refined: lace curtains at the windows and antimacassars on the sofa.

grisly/grizzly

One of the best-liked and most admired reporters of The New York Times is R. W. "Johnny" Apple, for many years head of the paper's London bureau. He filed one startling dispatch about a coal town in Wales that nurses bitter memories of disasters in the mines. "It is, in a way, a grizzly heritage."

The redoubtable Johnny surely wrote *grisly*, for a grizzly heritage in Wales would certainly bear watching, but transoceanic typesetting is a risky business.

hail/hale

A notion persists, especially among young reporters just beginning to cover the courts, that people are *hailed* into court. They're not. Defendants or reluctant witnesses are *haled*—that is, they are compelled to show up.

To *hail* is to salute, pay tribute to, or in the case of a taxi or a passing ship, to flag it down. In Manhattan at five o'clock in the afternoon, taxis provide a hail of a way to get across town.

hairlipped/harelipped

This isn't a true homophone, because there's no such word as *hairlipped*, but the misspelling of *harelipped* is so frequent that a brief reminder may not be amiss. The fifteenth-century word applies to a congenital deformity that causes the upper lip to be split as a hare's lip is split. When the Portland Oregonian once spoke of "surgery for hairlipped persons," it evoked an image of a gleaming scalpel and a short mustache.

hardy/hearty

The U.S. Bureau of Land Management publishes a regional newsletter for Oregon and Washington. The issue for August 1984 had one of those headlines that provoke a question of how's that again? "Hearty Weeds Make Area Difficult to Restock." The author meant to speak of *hardy* weeds, meaning those weeds that can survive almost any attempts at eradication, but *hardy* and *hearty* aren't so very far apart. A hearty fellow is a robust and vigorous fellow; a hearty meal is an abundant meal; hearty greetings are exuberant greetings. All this sounds remarkably like my dandelions.

heal/heel

To write that someone is well-*healed* is to suggest that the person is recovering satisfactorily from an illness or operation. The well-*heeled* person, in the idiomatic phrase, is well-to-do, prosperous, in the money. Heal is always a verb; it has one meaning only. We heal a wound, or heal a broken heart, or heal a relationship. We mend it. But *heel* is all kinds of things. It is the back of your foot, the end crust of bread, the bottom of a pole, the base of a ladder, or a downright contemptible cad. As a verb, *heel* has well-understood meanings for ships and dogs and shoemakers. To be down-at-the-heels is to look shabby or unkempt.

hear/here

No grown-up should confuse *hear* and *here*, but a reporter in La Grande, Ore., managed to do it. Twenty-five German students, busily touring the state, "got a chance to walk eight miles of the Old Oregon Trail near hear."

Anyone who is the least bit uncertain needs only to remember that we hear with our ears.

heard/herd

The details of the matter remain obscure, but down in southwest Virginia a dozen children had to be transported to serve as witnesses in the trial of a criminal case in a nearby county. Reported the Roanoke Times & World-News: "Commonwealth's Attorney Don Caldwell had toyed with the idea of sending a secretary along to ride heard over the children, but decided the sheriff's deputies driving the vans could do double duty."

A bus of noisy children might constitute a heard of children, but the wanted word here was *herd*. (Children are

not supposed to be herd; they are supposed only to be seen.) Webster's defines *herd* as "a number of animals of one kind." Fair enough, but in ordinary usage *herd* applies literally only to animals of the four-legged kind—cattle, pigs, buffalo, elephants, and the like. Theodore Bernstein is authority for a *herd of cranes* and a *herd of wrens*, but you would have to be awfully deep in ornithology to insist on these puristic usages. (Bernstein also sanctions a *herd of swans* and a *herd of whales*; in my book swans come in wedges and whales in pods or schools.) I seem to be digressing. The sheriff's deputies in Virginia were riding herd.

heroin/heroine

The Blue Valley High School in Johnson County, Kan., put on a production of the sawdust melodrama, *The Curse of an Aching Heart*. The Olathe Daily News quoted director Roger Shepard:

"Hopefully, we'll get audience participation, booing the villain, cheering the hero, and aahing for the heroin."

An unidentified paper in Florida carried an editorial denouncing higher-ups in the narcotics racket. In a passionate conclusion, the editor declared that "the electric chair is too good for heroine smugglers. They ought to be hanged."

In the Roanoke Times & World-News, a book reviewer outlined the plot of a novel: It involved "an international heroine smuggling ring."

What a difference an *e* makes! It is heroin dealers we despise and hoop-skirted heroines we applaud. One might well find something good to say of a smuggler of heroines. There's always room for a few more of those.

hew / hue

A writer in The Wall Street Journal recalled the protests that erupted when it transpired that the Soviet Union had developed and deployed a missile known as the SS-19. "The incident brought on a hew and cry in the U.S. and taught Moscow a lesson."

It's unlikely that *hew* and *hue* will often be confused, for *hew* isn't even a noun, but *hue and cry* carries such vivid echoes of long-ago England that it merits a digressive word. In the thirteenth century, a *hue and cry* summoned villagers to the pursuit of a fleeing felon. Somewhat later it became a formal proclamation for the capture of a fugitive; the reward notices that once were posted in our railway stations and post offices were announcements of hue and cry. These days, a bit worn at the edges, the phrase conveys only a general sense of alarm and commotion.

hoard / horde

The Columbus (Ohio) Dispatch put together a feature story on the famed Brookstone retail stores and catalog warehouses. Where do the hardware magnates find all those wonderful gadgets? The area manager explained that Brookstone maintains a staff of buyers who travel worldwide. "They come back with hoards of potential products."

The Omaha World-Herald had a solid editorial opinion early in 1985: "One thing U.S. and Soviet negotiators definitely don't need when arms talks resume in Geneva is a hoard of U.S. senators and congressmen looking over the negotiators' shoulders."

The Bloomington (Ind.) Herald-Telephone assigned a staff writer to cover the basketball trials that preceded the Olympics of 1984. The reporter was awed by the visiting press. He wrote that a whole "herd of journalists" had signed in, but that wasn't the way the phrase came out in the headline: "Hoard of Journalists Pursuing Olympic Basketball Trials."

A columnist in the Daily Review of Hayward, Calif., made a series of resolutions for taking better care of her beloved but ailing old car. The vehicle, name of Lemon, was suffering chiefly from a kind of asthma, brought on by a nervous carburetor. In times past the columnist had written about Lemon's deficiencies, but the publicity had caused Lemon to weep in her muffler. Very well, the columnist resolved, "While I am permitted to horde repair bills, I am not to continue sending same to various consumer publications."

Webster's says that *horde* is of Mongolian origin, and in its original sense applied to tribes of Mongolian nomads. By extension, a horde has become a kind of herd; it is a swarm, a throng, or a crowd.

A *hoard* is something else. It is a hidden supply of something. We hoard gold, or canned goods, or precious memories. The nuances go to secrecy, and in some contexts to selfishness or greed. It is socially okay to build up reserves, but to hoard a supply is not much admired.

home/hone

In January 1985, rescue workers searched a part of Hamilton County, Tenn., looking for a downed airplane. The Chattanooga Times reported that a powerful radio signal had been detected in the area. Thirty volunteers and three airplanes "tried to hone in on the signal, thought to be coming from an emergency locater transmitter."

"Hone in" sounds right, but it isn't. The verb is *home in.* That's about the only form in which the verb is used these days. To say that a lost dog *homed* would sound odd, but among pigeon fanciers it probably remains a term of art. Pigeons don't fly home, they *home.* To *hone* something is to sharpen it.

hurdle/hurtle

On Long Island, a career criminal who was serving time in the Suffolk County Jail for a minor offense learned that he was about to be indicted on felony charges.

"He tried an escape," reported Newsday, "managing to unravel the wires in two chain link fences, then hurtle an outer fence."

It was the trick of the week. When we hurtle something—a discus, a baseball bat, a ripe tomato—we throw it. Any man who can throw an outer fence ought to have a career on the playing fields. Presumably the reporter was thinking of *hurdle,* but that probably wasn't the right word either. A hurdle for horses might be six feet high, but a hurdle for humans is a relatively low barrier. The prisoner just climbed over that outer fence.

impugn/impute

Columnist Tom Braden, ordinarily a fan of the Rev. Jesse Jackson, became at least temporarily disenchanted when Jackson criticized Israel's rescue of starving black Jews in

Ethiopia. "Why impute the motives of those who are engaged in a humanitarian act?" asked Braden. "Maybe it will occur to Jackson some day that it is impossible to want to see America as a rainbow coalition and at the same time impute the motives of millions of Americans who want to help their co-religionists in foreign lands."

To *impute* is to attribute, often in a sense of blaming or accusing; we impute bad motives to the Watergate burglars. To *impugn* is to challenge, to attack, to assail with arguments; Jackson impugned the Israelis' motives by saying the rescue was in essence a "military mission."

incredible / incredulous

"Developments in the New Bedford, Mass., gang rape trial," proclaimed a Midwestern editorial, "were incredulous to say the least."

In Alabama, a retiring county commissioner spoke in a farewell statement of the low salaries paid to public officials. Said the Press-Register in Mobile: "He thinks low public salaries are incredulous."

The writers didn't mean *incredulous*; they meant *incredible*, but the words are brother and sister and the dictionaries are of little help in keeping them apart. To get at the difference, you have to start with *credulity* and *credulous*. To speak of someone's credulity is to speak of his capacity to believe; such a person is credulous—but with this important qualification: The belief, whatever it is, rests upon flimsy evidence. To believe in late October of 1984 that Walter Mondale would win the presidency would have tested anyone's credulity. Only a few credulous followers believed any such thing. To believe in the astrology columns—those half-baked compendiums of fortune cookies—also would test one's credulity. Many of the promises of politicians leave us incredulous.

Credibility and *credible* are something else. Here we are talking about a capacity to believe that is based upon a reasonable sufficiency of evidence. In a newspaper, credibility rests in the paper's reputation for accuracy and integrity. When a publication loses its credibility—even a little piece of its credibility—the damage takes a long time to repair. Ask the publishers of The Washington Post, The Wall Street Journal, and The New Yorker magazine.

In writing about the rape case, the editor meant to say that developments at the close of the trial were amazing, astonishing, fantastic, unbelievable, but "developments," having no capacity to believe anything, could not be *incredulous*. They were incredible, yes, but only people are incredulous.

inciteful / insightful

There's no such word as *inciteful*, but it turned up anyhow in a letter addressed to fellow members of the Order of the Coif at the University of Pennsylvania Law School. The chapter president advised members that Lloyd Cutler, White House counsel during the Carter years, would give a lecture. "Those of us who know Mr. Cutler know you will find him an inciteful, exciting speaker."

Bosh. Some of us who remember Lloyd Cutler from the Carter years remember him as a man of reason, dignity, and reserve—not the type to incite a rabble to storm the barricades. But even *inciteful* is better in every way than *insightful*, which is what the president of Coif intended. *Insightful*, meaning to be full of insights, is an abominable word. It ought to be put with *meaningful* in a lead casket and dropped overboard without ceremony in the sea of words.

interment / internment

In the Daily Leader of Brookhaven, Mass., readers found some puzzling information about the day's funeral arrangements: "Internments will follow at Rose Hill and Newsight Cemeteries."

And perhaps residencies would follow the internments. The needed word was *interments*, which comes to us by Federal Express straight from the Latin *in terra*, in the earth. At one time both *to bury* and *to inter*, in their funereal meanings, conveyed the idea of placing a body in a grave. Contemporary usage sanctions "above-ground burial" in mausoleums or other tombs.

its/it's

In the letters column of a community newspaper in Louisville, a civic leader expressed thanks for contributions to the Exploited Children's Help Organization. The charity "has recently been given a boost in it's effort to combat child exploitation by the Younger Woman's Club of Louisville."

Well, shame on the Younger Woman's Club of Louisville! And shame on the author of the letter for confusing *it's* and *its*. Shame on all of us, including me, who by sheer inattention once wrote of the word *lagniappe* that "it's roots are in Spanish, not in French." I actually did that. It can happen to everybody, but it ought not to happen to anybody. Let us watch these contractions closely, and let us pray that the public schools will teach their pupils the difference between contractions and possessives. The most modest recasting would have given us: "The Exploited Children's Help Organization recently has been given a boost by the Younger Woman's Club of Louisville in its efforts to combat child exploitation." The sentence now is tickety-boo, and the recasting took maybe five seconds.

jibe/jive

A headline in the Spokane Chronicle added a little swing to a not very jazzy proceeding: "Information Given Audit Committee Doesn't Jive with Testimony."

A newspaper published by the Assemblies of God and distributed in Washington state retold the story of the arraignment of Jesus before Caiaphas (Matthew 26). Two false witnesses were found to testify against Jesus, "but their stories didn't jive."

The word is *jibe*. Webster's dates it from 1813, but finds the origin unknown. It means simply to agree with. As for *jive*, it means to tease or kid along, or to dance in ways that sexagenarians may not fully appreciate. Neither of these should be confused with *gibe*, which means to taunt.

juggler/jugular

Toward the end of the presidential campaign of 1984, the Charleston (W.Va.) Gazette delighted lovers of bad vaudeville with a memorable headline:

Reagan Goes
For Juggler
In Midwest

Who was this clumsy fellow who had aroused the president's ire? Some fumbler of duckpins? Some dropper of plates? Alas, Mr. Reagan was not pursuing an incompetent juggler. He was going for the jugular of the Democrats, but the Republicans had no monopoly on the exercise. The Youngstown Vindicator speculated in August 1984 that Geraldine Ferraro would "go for the juggler on the fierce give-and-take a nationwide TV audience will bring out."

For the record, and contrary to a popular notion, there isn't just one jugular vein. There are several jugulars on each side of the neck; their function is to return blood from the brain. Because this function is vital, *jugular* long ago became a metaphor for the most vulnerable part of anything. It's hard to tell, looking back at the '84 campaign, what was Mr. Mondale's most vulnerable point. Save in the District of Columbia and Minnesota, the poor fellow was vulnerable everywhere.

lam/lamb

A resident of Morgantown, Ind., couldn't believe his eyes when he awoke at three o'clock on a Sunday morning to see what he thought was a monkey running through his backyard. Sure enough, it was a monkey—one of three that had escaped from a zoo in Nashville, 250 miles away. Reported the Columbus (Ind.) Republic: "Owner Tom Tilton said the monkey, which weighs about thirty pounds, had been on the lamb since Aug. 21."

That interesting information certainly improves the story. It is a sufficiently eye-opening experience to awake at three a.m. to see a monkey in the yard, but a monkey on the lamb? It baffles belief. Webster's dates *lam*, which is what this elusive anthropoid in fact was on, from 1897. There also is a transitive verb, *to lam*, that etymologists trace to 1596 in the sense of to beat or to thrash. The intransitive *lam* means "to flee hastily," but the verb is rarely used. Nobody lams any more. Except in bad gangster

movies and Indiana feature stories, nobody ever goes on the lam.

lamas/llamas

Columnist Nick Thimmesch early in 1985 came up with a startling lead: "Ronald Reagan is the first president in my memory to take on the llamas of the so-called civil rights movement." Probably it was no more than an *l* of a typographical error, but it conjured a vision of the president meeting with a herd of camel-like creatures at some summit in the Andes. The two-*l* llama has four legs, the one-*l* lama, a Tibetan monk, has but two.

lay/lie

Are any two verbs in English more often confused than *lay* and *lie*? I know of none. Two lamentable examples may suffice:

In a review for the Indianapolis Star, an associate professor of journalism, alas, outlined the plot of Roger Vadim's novel, *The Hungry Angel*. Two young actors, Julian and Sophie, fall in love, but she suffers a paralyzing injury. He remains her lover, but "Julian roams afield while Sophie lays and writes."

An ad of the J. C. Penney Company, in an unidentified paper, promotes a bargain in bathing suits: "Choose from one to two pieces in all the new exciting styles for the beach or just laying in the sun."

The best device for keeping these critters straight is to remember that we *lay* bricks and we *lie* down. Apart from a couple of exceptions, *lay* always takes an object; *lie* never does. Thus a mason lays bricks, a gambler lays bets, and a chicken lays eggs. When these things have been done, the bricks, the bets, and the eggs have been *laid*.

The problem rests in the perversity of *lie* in the past tense: We *lay* down; we have *lain* down. A sportswriter in Roanoke wrote of some weary basketball players; during a time-out "they laid on the floor." One had to ask, what did they lay on the floor? The writer wanted the simple past tense of *to lie*. The players *lay* on the floor.

leach/leech

These are trickers—tricky enough to throw writers on such eminent publications as Field & Stream and The New York Times.

The magazine informed its readers that deer have been getting smaller along coastal areas, and this is especially true "where the soil is mainly made up of leeched sand."

The Times had a story about a coal-fired plant of the Montana Power Company. Its waste materials affect the Kluver ranch. "Mrs. Kluver believes toxic metals from that waste are leeching through the soil and into the ground water."

In each instance, the writer wanted *leach*, not *leech*. The process of *leaching* involves the separation of a solid from its solution by a process of percolation. You can leach ashes; you can leach sand. The process of *leeching*, long since abandoned in the medical world, involves the use of a leech—an ugly worm if ever there was one—to suck blood. By extension, a human leech is one who leeches on to another person. Sailors know leeches as the vertical edges of square sails, but that has nothing to do with the confusion at hand.

liable/likely

Parade magazine had an article on phobias—phobias about ants, bats, and elevators, and phobias about baths, planes, and public speeches. One woman had a phobia about dogs, but her terror was totally disproportionate, "since the dogs she was liable to encounter represented no danger."

Wrong word. We needed to know about the dogs she was *likely* to encounter. In the sense sought here, the adjective *liable* means to be exposed to some regrettable contingency or risk. In the sense of responsibility, we may be *liable* for damages. If the woman were bitten by a dog, she might be *liable* to rabies.

The simple and uncomplicated *likely* suggests probability, nothing more. The dogs the woman probably would encounter represented no danger. Depending upon the probabilities, it may be likely to snow tomorrow. If it does snow, persons who go out and get chilled may be liable to pneumonia. And if they don't shovel hard, they may be *liable* to getting stuck.

linch/lynch

During the primary campaigns of 1984 the Lubbock (Texas) Evening Journal scolded Walter Mondale for an inadequate answer to a question raised by Reubin Askew. The issue had to do with Mondale's support of a multimillion-dollar gas pipeline in Alaska. Mondale said he always had opposed the concept of pre-billing prospective customers to raise capital, but pre-billing, said the Journal, "was the lynchpin of the pipeline's entire financial plan."

The preferred spelling is *linchpin*. It's the locking pin inserted through a hole in an axle that keeps the wheel from falling off. By metaphorical extension, it is the thing that holds all elements together. A cotter pin, which appeared in the 1880s, is a form of linchpin. The variant spelling of *lynchpin* carries ugly connotations and might well be abandoned.

load / lode

A paper in Kansas gave me such a nice review of a book of mine that I haven't the heart to identify the publication. The reviewer commented generously that "any writer who picks up the book has hit a motherload."

Ah, no. This agreeable critic meant *motherlode*, a rich deposit of ore. A motherload might be composed of a baby on each hip and a tote bag of diapers. One of my daughters-in-law carries in her van a motherload of Girl Scouts.

loose / lose

Even on well-edited papers—papers as well edited as the Christian Science Monitor—the *loose/lose* gremlin has a way of creeping into print. The Monitor quoted an ecologist on the damage that fire can do in a tropical rain forest. Such a forest "is an extremely delicate ecosystem and like loosing an arm, the rest of the body is bound to be affected."

There's nothing wrong with *loose* as a verb. An archer looses an arrow; a woman looses her long hair. But only a wrestler could loose an arm.

magnate / magnet

Jim Forbes, a thirty-six-year-old accountant from Winter Haven, Fla., won a much coveted prize at Los Angeles in 1984. He wasn't in the Olympics; he was playing against four opponents to become U.S. Monopoly champion. The L.A. Times/Washington Post Service interviewed the champ, and noted that Mr. Forbes is "no relation to magazine magnet Malcolm S. Forbes."

Those who have had the good fortune to meet Malcolm Forbes will testify that the gentleman is indeed a magnetic personality; like all balloonists and bike riders, he's also a little bit nuts. But in the publishing world he's not a *magnet*; he's a *magnate*, out of the Latin for *great*.

mail / male

The etymologists say that *mail* comes from a Scottish word for sack or bag, which sounds plausible. A bundle of letters would be put in a bag of some kind, and the fellow who carried the bag naturally would be known as the *mailman*. There's another *mail* also, meaning armor made of small metal links, but that isn't a mail you'll often meet in the morning paper.

J. T. Harding, the New Jersey logomachist, has several citations of such confusions as *male box*, *male carrier*, and *male clerk*, which certainly would be a puzzler if the mail clerk were female.

marshal / martial

When a key Democratic senator had to be hospitalized with heart surgery, the president of the Ohio state Senate gave up on a redistricting bill. Sen. Henry Meshel told the Miami Valley Sunday News that "he will make no attempt to martial his 17-16 majority for a political finale at the expense of Ocasek's health."

You don't often see the adjective *martial* mixed up with the verb *to marshal*, but these things happen. When we *marshal* something—troops, facts, evidence—we do more than merely bring them together. The connotation is of a neat, orderly, and regular assembling. The noun *marshal* may be spelled with two *l*s, but the preferred spelling is with one. The Florence (S.C.) Morning News once reported on a Fourth of July parade under the supervision of Grand Marshal William Burns. "He'll be leading off the celebration in a fire truck dressed as Uncle Sam." They do have colorful times in Florence, S.C.

As for *martial*, meaning warlike, the usual confusion results from typographical error. The marital troubles of Elizabeth Taylor have a regrettable way of appearing in print as her martial troubles instead.

memento/momento

The Island Packet, a weekly published at Hilton Head Island, S.C., carried a streamer headline over a book review: "A Hemingway Momento for Writers, Fishermen."

Webster's Ninth New Collegiate, tut-tut, sanctions *momento* as a variant of *memento*, but neither Random House nor American Heritage, to their credit, pays any attention to this barbarism. The only acceptable version is *memento*, something that prompts memory.

militate/mitigate

Even The New York Times can run afoul of these homophones. The Times once wondered whether an orchestra conductor, moving to the West Coast, would find that "the leisure-time orientation of Los Angeles itself mitigates against excellence."

Another well-edited paper, The Miami Herald, had the same problem: "One factor that could mitigate against merging Mickey Mouse with the mayor's dream is the city's schedule for selecting a Watson Island developer."

What the writers wanted was *militate*, which is to affect or to influence. In theory one could militate *for* a particular purpose, but the verb is used so universally in the sense of militate *against* that it carries a heavy connotation of an adverse effect.

The troublesome *mitigate* means to relieve, mollify, ameliorate, make less onerous. To mitigate damages is to reduce them.

moot/mute

Clemson University's football team won its first two games in 1984, and then lost two in a row to Georgia and Georgia Tech. The defeats resulted from interceptions and fumbles. Quarterback Mike Eppley speculated that without the turnovers the record probably would be 4-0. Commented a sportswriter for The Greenville (S.C.) News: "That's a good bet on a mute point."

The quarterback surely wasn't whooping it up for a 2-2 record, but the point wasn't *mute*; it was *moot*. To be mute is to be speechless. *Moot* is a tricker, one of a handful of words known as contranyms. It can mean both "open to argument" and "no longer open to argument." In ordinary usage, a moot point is an arguable point; at the Supreme Court, when a case is dismissed as moot, it means there no longer is an issue to argue about.

morays/mores

The Lubbock (Texas) Avalanche-Journal interviewed the author of a book about serial killings. He thought these crimes "conceivably can be traced back to attitudes of the 1960s and early 1970s with free-wheeling morays . . ."

The Chicago Tribune had a startling summary of the movie *Swann in Love*. The film focuses on "an upper-class

MORAYS OF THE COMPANY

Jew in 19th century Paris who clashes with contemporary morays when he falls in love with a prostitute."

The magazine Security World reviewed some research on employee theft. Two scholars from the University of Minnesota had concluded that such thefts are best understood "as a function of the overall work environment and the social patterns and morays of the company."

Never mind the Orkin Man! Summon the ichthyologists! It might be better to have a few thieving employees than to have some morays around the office. The lost word was *mores*. The preferred pronunciation is *mo-rays*, but it's also heard as *more-ease*. In any event it means "the fixed morally binding customs of a particular group." Contemporary *morays* would be fresh-caught eels of an especially vicious variety. Says Webster's: Such eels can inflict "a savage bite."

muscle / mussel / muzzle

The Northwest Orient Airlines' magazine carried a feature article on a famous sushi chef, name of Hiroshi, and reported that he "enjoys Spanish Sangria and muscles marinara."

The Miami Herald carried a nice feature on seafood, complete with a drawing of four succulent bivalves. Alas, these were identified in a cutline as "sample muscles from the South Pacific."

The Cumberland (Md.) News advised readers that owing to inclement March weather, "The shoot set Sunday afternoon by the Western Maryland Mussel Loaders Association has been canceled."

The Japanese chef hadn't gone cannibalistic; he was fond of *mussels*, not *muscles*. That's what those South Pacific bivalves were: They were *mussels*. But in Maryland the gun lovers were loading guns through their *muzzles*. It will serve only to add to the confusion to note that *mussel* stems from the Latin *musculus* and Middle English *muscle*. As for *muzzle*, it has to do with the mouth or snout of an animal—by extension, the open end of a firearm.

naval / navel

Some years ago a young journalist sought a grant from the Fund for Investigative Journalism. He thought something fishy was going on in navel purchasing. He saw scandals in navel procurement. He suspected collusion on the part of high-ranking navel officers. Alas, he got no grant.

The seagoing word is *naval*. The belly button is a *navel*. To write of a "navel battle" would suggest a hot competition at the Nile Hilton among Cairo's finest dancers.

nitpicking / knitpicking

Erma Bombeck probably had it right to begin with, but as her column appeared in the Mt. Airy (N.C.) News, it sounded a little odd. She was brushing off complaints about how people handle their toothpaste tubes. "I'm not one of those hysterical, knit-picking perfectionists," she said.

A knitpicker might be someone who picks those tiny balls of fuzz off a wool sweater, but *nits* are louse eggs or lice themselves. In passing, English has only seven or eight nouns that end in *ouse*—blouse, grouse, house, louse, souse, spouse. Foreigners who set out to learn English must wonder why the plurals are blouses, grouse, houses, lice, mice, souses, and spouses.

oar / o'er / or / ore

Conceivably someone might confuse *oar* and *ore*, but you'd have to try hard. I throw it in only because it's a four-way homophone, and deserves a salute in passing.

paddies / patties

Actors Ken Wahl and Cheryl Ladd made a movie called *Purple Hearts*. The movie is a romance, said The Miami Herald, "set in the rice patties and firing zones of wartime Vietnam."

If you mix leftover rice with an egg, maybe you'd get rice patties (if you mix rice with black-eyed peas you get hopping John), but those marshy swamps in Vietnam were *paddies*. In the puristic view it's redundant to speak of a *rice* paddy because there isn't any other kind of paddy, but if the modifying *rice* materially assists a reader's comprehension, it's not a federal offense to leave it in.

pail / pale

William Safire, whose column "On Language" delights readers of the Sunday New York Times Magazine, got off a neat play on words in a discussion of parliamentary speech. He said that a denunciation of Sen. Homer Capehart as "a rancid tub of ignorance" was "beyond the pail."

In his column a week later, just to prove he was only teasing, he remarked that when George Bush imputed a lack of patriotism to critics of the Marines in Lebanon, this was generally considered "beyond the pale of political debate."

BEYOND THE PAIL OF POLITICAL DEBATE

I once got to kidding around in print and said that *beyond the pale* came from the small ring around the cup in the ancient game of tiddlywinks. If a wink fell beyond the ring, it was "beyond the pale," out of bounds, and not to be countenanced. Some folks bought that foolishness. In serious etymology, *pale* comes from the same roots that give us *palisade*. A pale is a picket or sharpened stake; when we fasten pales together we get a fence or boundary. Beyond the pale thus means beyond the fence. In 1984 Tony Armas of the Red Sox hit forty-three balls beyond the pale.

pair/pare

In Spokane, Wash., 140 men and women competed in tryouts for the Olympic cycling teams. At the end of the day only the best survived. In Naples, Fla., the Daily News told about it in a headline: "U.S. Cyclists Paired to Dozen."

A couple of other *-air* homophones also give trouble (*fair/fare* and *hair/hare*), but the *pair/pare* confusion occurs most frequently. The field of cyclists was *pared* down; it was trimmed down by removing the excess on the edges.

parity/parody

A columnist in Our Sunday Visitor undertook to analyze Ronald Reagan's views on strategic arms: "He wants the Republican platform, for example, to support nuclear parody with the Soviet Union, not U.S. nuclear superiority."

In Marion, Ind., the Chronicle-Tribune looked at a major public expense—the cost of maintaining "teachers' wage scale parody."

No laughing matters, these. A *parody* is a comic imitation of something else, e.g., a poem, a song, a mannerism, a style of speaking or writing. As for *parity*, it means the general state of being equal, but in terms of farmers' income and commodity price supports, no man alive can explain what parity means. Farm parity is a mystery that must be accepted on faith, like loaves, fishes, and the Holy Ghost.

partially / partly

Once upon a time there lived in the city room of a Virginia newspaper a managing editor who had a really terrible thing about *partly* and *partially*. If you mixed them up you could spoil his whole day. And he could spoil yours. As soon as a reporter wrote that a particular program had been "partially financed" by federal funds, Mr. Hamilton (for that was the editor's name) would come roaring out of his office.

"*Partly* financed!" he would cry. He was in anguish. "*Partly* financed!"

Nothing was to be gained by pointing out to this venerable gentleman that the most reputable dictionaries define *partial* as meaning *in part;* and these same dictionaries also define *partly* as meaning *partial.* My mentor Hamilton was right, as he practically always was. *Partial* carries an immediate meaning of biased, or prejudiced, or markedly in favor of one person or position as opposed to another. We can be partial to labor, or partial to business or partial to ice cream or spinach, but we could never be *partly* to any of these. I would reserve *partial* for occasions involving favoritism or preference, and save *partly* for those occasions when all we mean is *in part.*

partition / petition

In Winter Haven, Fla., the Red Lobster restaurant set aside about a third of its 250 seats for non-smokers. Manager Jim Kelly told the Lakeland Ledger that the move had worked out happily: "The gallery has been petitioned off, and everybody loves it who uses it."

In Mobile, Zundel's Jewelry Store moved from the north arcade of Springfield Plaza Mall to the front of the shopping area. Reported the morning Register: "Walls and petitions between two stores were removed to create the larger store."

Perhaps if the restaurant management had acted upon a

petition from nonsmoking patrons, the gallery might have been truly "petitioned off," but in these instances Red Lobster was putting partitions up and Zundel's was taking them down. A *petition* is a serious written entreaty for a particular purpose. A *partition* is a division or a separation, whether of a parcel of land or of space within a structure.

passed/past

Opening Day in Seattle is a big event. Reported the Times: "From the parade of boats sailing passed thousands of spectators and crafts to the 3,000 runners who raced across the Evergreen Point floating bridge, the day was a chance to welcome the arrival of spring and the yachting season."

The staff reporter was nodding. The boats *passed* the spectators but they sailed *past* them. No one who pays attention to what he is writing is going to confuse the verb and the preposition, but sometimes, alas, we do not pay attention.

peace/piece

In Reading, Pa., the local gas company distributed a flier promoting its service contracts: "For piece of mind, fill in and return the coupon below."

In San Antonio, the AP reported that a prisoner named Meeks abandoned a fifty-two-day fast after being given an opportunity to testify before a grand jury. Said Meeks' attorney: "I think it's simply because he was elated that the grand jury allowed him to say his peace."

The nouns were backward here. A utility that offers its customers "piece of mind" is likely to get a piece of their mind in return. As for "saying his peace," what this prisoner was doing was saying his piece.

peak / peek / pique

Slowly, slowly. Let us creep up on this impish threesome slowly. A sportswriter for the Tallahassee Democrat was invited to serve as a judge in a bikini contest. He chastely declined, but allowed that "I might take a few peaks."

A writer for Time magazine had the same idea. In a piece on videocassette players, he noted that X-rated movies make up about 15 percent of rentals. "Many VCR owners who would not go near a downtown porno theater will sneak a peak at X-rated tapes in the discreet environs of their own homes."

The Chicago Tribune summed up a bleak week in March: "During the past week the sun only peaked down on Chicago for a total of fifty minutes." Things were better in April off the New Jersey coast. Said the Asbury Park Press: "It doesn't take much sunshine to peak through the clouds to attract die-hard surfers . . ."

In Oregon, the Grants Pass Daily Courier summarized the plot of a soap opera: "When Kirby collapsed, a panicked Adam came to her aid, peaking Blake's curiosity." The AP traced the history of a baseball trade between Philadelphia and Detroit; when the Tigers said they might be willing to part not only with catcher John Wockenfuss but also with outfielder Glenn Wilson, "that peaked Philadelphia's interest."

Boston had the same experience. In Bostonia magazine, editor-in-chief Laura Freid observed that "narrative stories of human events, whether they are of failure or of success, peak our interest."

In the Lancaster (Pa.) New Era, readers learned of a family feud that had taken the lives of two brothers within two months. "Police said the long-running feud between the Coward and Woods families piqued Thursday night when a woman had her nose broken . . ."

Aaargh! Confusion now hath made his masterpiece. Let us attempt a disentanglement.

PEAK / PEEK / PIQUE

Peak, the noun, is the top of a hill or a mountain. By extension, it is the highest level or greatest degree of practically anything. The verb conveys the idea of reaching the maximum point: The wind *peaked* at 60 miles per hour. (It may not clarify, and may only add to the confusion, to note that *peak* is contranymic; it can mean *to reach the top*, but it also can mean *to grow sickly* or *to dwindle away*. From this latter meaning we derive the two-syllable *peak-ed*, for someone who looks pale and wan.)

Peek, the noun, is what the Florida sportswriter was going to take a few of. It is a glance, a brief look. In some contexts *peek* carries a connotation of furtiveness. The VCR owners were sneaking peeks. In Chicago and in New Jersey the sun was peeking down; it was appearing for a few minutes, only to be obscured by clouds. Brevity is the soul of a peek.

Pique, the noun, is a snit, a little spasm of wounded pride or resentment. As a verb, it can mean *to annoy* or *to irritate*, but more often it means *to arouse* or *to challenge*.

On the soap opera, curiosity was piqued; in Boston and in Philadelphia, interest was piqued. To be sure, if interest gradually were aroused, it could be said that at some point interest peaked, but let it go.

peal / peel

From Los Angeles, the AP reported the opening of the Olympic Games: "Church bells peeled at the start of the ceremonies."

In Washington, D.C., the AP reported a White House tribute to prisoners of war in Vietnam: "At the conclusion of the ceremony, four Navy F-14 Tomcats flew overhead in the 'missing man' formation, with one plane pealing off to fly skyward representing a fallen soldier."

In the Peoria, Ill., Journal Star, Dr. Paul Donohue warned a reader against overuse of vitamin A: "It can cause pealing of the skin, bone tenderness, and liver damage."

Whether as noun or verb, *peal* has a narrow meaning. It conveys the idea of loudness and usually of a succession of loud sounds. Church bells *peal*: They ring loudly. Bells might *ring* softly, but they couldn't *peal* softly. A person conceivably might give vent to only one peal of laughter, but ordinarily such laughter comes in the plural.

Peel is a little more versatile. A *peel*, first off, is the skin or rind of a fruit or vegetable; it is also a label on a can or the backing on certain film or gummed labels. In less familiar contexts, a peel also is a stockade and a baker's long-handled tool for getting bread out of an oven. The verb always conveys the idea of taking off an outer layer. We peel a potato; we peel off a sweater. In that aerial formation, the plane peeled off.

It may help to recall that the ringing of a bell is a kind of summons—an appeal to assemble. The linguistic root that gives us *peal* also produces such twigs as *appeal* and *appellate*. Webster's traces *peel* to the Latin *pilus*, hair, from which we also get *pile* in the sense of that velvety surface on new blankets or carpets.

pedal/peddle

In the letters column of the Fort Pierce (Fla.) News Tribune, an angry reader vented his wrath upon agents of the Internal Revenue Service. Their principal task, he said, is "pedalling fear."

In Peking, the AP quoted a Western diplomat on China's pledge to maintain a system of free enterprise in Hong Kong: "This is a concrete example of the soft-line approach they have been pedaling since 1978."

In Washington, the AP quoted Congressman James A. Courter of New Jersey on the Soviet Union's recent violations of arms treaties: "I think that the administration is soft-peddling the issue."

In Eufaula, Ala., the weekly Tribune covered the story of nineteen bike riders, known as the Christian Wayfarers, who passed through town after traveling by bus from Michigan to Florida. "The youths will peddle the rest of the way back to Michigan."

Those agents of the IRS weren't pedaling fear; they were peddling fear. That was what the Chinese were doing also; they were peddling a soft-line approach, selling it to anyone who would buy the proposition. The verb goes back to the sixteenth century; it conveys the idea of hawking one's wares from place to place.

If he traveled by bicycle or pedicab, a peddler might *pedal* his way. The noun and the verb grow from the Latin word for foot. Such related nouns as *pedometer*, *pedicure*, and *pedestrian* have trod their way into English from the same starting point. Those youths were pedaling back to Michigan, and the Reagan administration, like a piano player, was soft-pedaling the issue.

pidgin/pigeon

In The Miami Herald, TV columnist Steve Sonsky had some harsh things to say about an NBC personality in New York who attempted to interview the defecting Chinese tennis player Hu Na. She was in Detroit, and the audio hookup was poor. The columnist described the fiasco:

" 'I can't hear. I can't hear. I'm sorry, I can't hear anything,' Hu said over and over in pigeon English . . ."

Was the defector a stoolie? Certainly not. The young woman was speaking *pidgin* English. (Webster's and American Heritage capitalize Pidgin English, but the Oxford American and Random House dictionaries sensibly leave it lowercased.) When Americans travel abroad, most of them speak—when they try to speak at all—a pidgin: Ou est le dining room? *Pigeon English* might be the jargon of informers.

plain/plane

"The bails of marijuana," read the news item, "were dropped from a low-flying plain." They weren't bails; they were bales, and what they were dropped from was a low-flying plane. The more frequent confusion has to do with *plain*, meaning simple, and *plane*, meaning flat. You might think that prairies, which are relatively flat grasslands, would be called "the planes," but they're not. They're the plains. A child's first course in geometry—the least complicated and simplest course—isn't plain geometry; it's plane geometry, as distinguished from solid geometry. On the other hand, plain speech is just that: simple speech, unadorned. Plane speech is the conversation of people who fly airplanes.

pole/poll

Florida's legislature passed a law in 1984 that ought to be widely emulated. The law requires candidates for public office, within thirty days after an election, to remove all signs promoting their candidacies. If the signs aren't removed in that period, city and county governments may do the job themselves and bill the candidates for the expense. The act was sponsored by state Rep. Bo Johnson of Gulf Breeze. His aide explained the background to The Miami Herald:

"Candidates were putting up signs in rights-of-way, on telephone polls, private property, trees, every place, and they'd hang there for weeks and weeks, until they rotted. It created a very ugly sight."

In Columbus, Ga., a headline writer for the Enquirer and Ledger stumbled into the same pitfall. It appeared from an AP story that Catherine Stevens was the only registrant in a precinct near Potter, N.Y., but her opportunity to cast her ballot would be preserved. "Poles to Open for Single Voter."

We do indeed have telephone polls, conducted by pollsters who are eager to know in election years what people will do at the polls. As verb or noun, *poll* derives from root words for head; when we take a poll we are counting heads. When we poll cattle, we cut off their horns. The offending political signs were fastened to poles that might or might not have been owned by the local telephone company; the poles might as readily have been owned by the electric power company. The Bell System people used to be sensitive on this point ("Six persons died Friday when their car smashed into a telephone pole"), but perhaps they have become reconciled to the generic nature of poles along streets and highways. In common parlance they're *all* telephone poles.

poor / pore / pour

Of all the homophones in English, none is more consistently abused than *pore* and *pour*. Now and then, a wandering *poor* comes by: The Journal and Courier of Lafayette,

Ind., carried a streamer headline, "Contributions Poor in for Ethiopians," but the greater confusions arise when we read that people pour over things. To wit:

The Washington Post had Penthouse publisher Bob Guccione and his assistant "pouring over 1,000 35mm slides of a woman in various degrees of dress and arousal." The Seattle Times had a convict "pouring over the food ads." Atlanta columnist Lewis Grizzard had Jimmy the Greek "pouring over his Racing Form." The Pillsbury people said in a house publication that their home economists were "pouring over a library's worth of food publications." During the trial of Patty Hearst, Time magazine spoke of her terrorist companions who "poured over floor plans and street maps." Columnist R. Emmett Tyrrell once had New York's Mayor Koch "pouring over the Bible to find a suitable passage." In the Winston-Salem (N.C.) Journal an amateur lexicographer "poured over the pages" of the OED with a magnifying glass. In the Brattleboro (Vt.) Reformer, an editorial writer was "pouring through business listings." In the Daily Record Chronicle of Renton, Wash., a headline writer summed up a continuing story: "Reagan Pours Over Options for Program Spending Cuts." Enough!

More than enough. If these several individuals actually had been *pouring*, Guccione would have had some wet slides, Jimmy the Greek a wet Racing Form, the terrorists some wet street maps, and Mayor Koch a soppy Bible. In every instance the desired verb was *pore*, which means to look at something intently. Its mischief-making cousin, *pour*, has to do with anything that flows in a continuous stream. A bartender pours drinks; a crowd pours into a stadium; a penitent pours out his confession.

poplar/popular

A garden columnist in the Augusta (Ga.) Chronicle ordered a couple of amaryllis bulbs by mail from Oregon. The bulbs arrived, but they didn't look like much. "Seeing the stubby green stalks, however, reminded my wife and me of the time we ordered through the mail two fast growing popular trees . . . Like our funny-looking popular trees, the amaryllis bulbs in due time started to grow leaves."

The gentleman's trees were *poplars*, a popular variety. They're part of the willow family.

principal/principle

It seems almost unfair to cite The Wall Street Journal on this homophonic tricker, but in October 1984, the Journal's "Money Matters" column set out to clarify what is meant by compounding interest. "If you think it's a simple matter of being paid interest on both accrued interest and principle, heed what happened last summer . . ."

Columnist Ann Landers—at least as her column appeared in the Portland Oregonian—had the same mishap. She heard from a woman whose husband had been hired and fired two dozen times in the past five years. Now his "principle occupation is trying to figure out ways to get unemployment compensation."

In The Washington Post, a writer on business affairs fouled his own nest: "The Washington Post Co. yesterday announced an agreement in principal to sell part of its interest in four regional cable television sports networks . . ."

The Journal's reporters know perfectly well that interest is paid on *principal*, not on principle, but somebody dozed while proof was being read. Ann Landers also knows that it was the fellow's principal occupation that had his wife upset. At the Post, while a multimillion-dollar transaction surely would involve large sums of principal, the agreement was an agreement *in principle*.

Somewhere there must be some effective mnemonic for keeping the words straight, but the lament of a misbehaving fourth-grader is not much help: "There ain't no 'pal' in 'principal.'" *Principal* is both noun and adjective; it always carries the meaning of something important or prominent—the principal of the trust, the principal reasons. Its confusing brother, *principle*, is a noun only; it has to do with underlying rules of conduct or function—the principle of states' rights, the principle that supports a judge's recusal. Webster's notes that *principal* and *principle* are often confused, and offers some sound advice: When in doubt, look 'em up in Webster's.

profit/prophet

Donald Lefton, chairman of a subcommittee to promote tourism in Miami Beach, may have been making a pun. It's hard to say. He was speaking at a symposium at which several speakers complained that no one listens to voices proclaiming the possibilities of the Beach. The city of Miami doesn't realize what the Beach has to offer, said one speaker. "We are a profit without honor in our own community," Lefton told the Miami Herald.

Well, ours is a world of sometimes honest profits and sometimes accurate prophets, and the disgruntled burghers of Miami Beach could be interpreted either way. The phrase to which the gentleman alluded is from Matthew 11:57—"a prophet is not without honor, save in his own country, and in his own house."

prostate/prostrate

The student newspaper at Washington State University noted in its personals column that a member of the faculty "had prostrate surgery on March 29." The Miami Herald, in a comparison of the candidates' health, noted that "Mondale's prostrate gland is slightly enlarged, but with no complications." In the Stuart (Fla.) News a 60-point headline offered some medical advice: "Prostrate Exams Important After Age 50."

In some surgical procedures, a patient may be in a *prostrate* position, i.e., lying flat with his face down, but in *prostate* surgery, no. The *prostate* is a gland at the base of the male urethra. To be *prostrate* is to be stretched out on the ground or on whatever surface one happens to be lying prone.

provincial

It isn't exactly a homophone—it's just a happy misspelling—but a classified ad in the Spokane Review held out new hope in the field of family planning:

> TWIN WHITE PREVENTIAL BEDS
> with box spring and mattress and
> matching bedspreads, $250.

Sell 'em to Kenya and Bangladesh! The natives may not have great use for Provincial beds, but with their birth rates, prevential beds might be just the thing.

rack/wrack

In September 1984 the sports editor of the Garden City (N.Y.) Telegram took a look at the first week of the football season: "The winners wracked up 471 points while the losers had just 56."

The word he wanted was *racked*. That is what you do with the balls in a game of pool: You put them in a rack. Metaphorically you can rack up almost anything—points, victories, losses, consecutive innings pitched without a walk. The homophone gives trouble because in other contexts *rack* is associated with pain, misery, or torture. In medieval days prisoners were broken on a rack, and it is from this meaning of *rack* that we get to *wrack*, as in "things are going to wrack and ruin." (Things seem never to go only to wrack or only to ruin; things always go to both.)

rain/reign/rein

In their search for corporate entrepreneurs, reported Venture magazine, "some companies have tried to give freer reign to their brightest people."

Reflecting upon the tough rule that Indira Gandhi imposed upon her people, the Clearwater (Fla.) Sun thought editorially that "perhaps it was the only way to hold the reigns of power in India, the largest democracy in the world."

In China, Deng Xiaoping announced that troops eventually would be stationed in Hong Kong. The Wall Street Journal's Peking correspondent thought the move was intended to placate military leaders. Mr. Deng also may have felt "the need to reign in other Chinese officials who have expressed views different from his own."

In Washington, the AP reported that "Consumer advocates told the government not to loosen the reigns barring American manufacturers from exporting dangerous products that have been recalled in this country."

REIN / REIGN / RAIN

At the News Guard in Lincoln City, Ore., a sportswriter named Jim David resigned; the headline over his farewell column read, "Honsowetz Assumes Reigns." At the Evening World in Bloomfield, Ind., a headline writer told us about a new quarterback for the Cleveland Browns: "McDonald Ready to Take Reigns."

Well, troubles rain, and confusion reigns, and top editors need to put reins on these offenders. For the record, *rain* is that wet stuff that falls from the sky; a *reign* is the period of a sovereign's rule; a *rein* is the leather strap with which one controls a horse. All three words come in both nouns and verbs, and all three crop up in metaphors all the time. A punster on the copy desk of the Lexington Herald delighted readers at the time Queen Elizabeth II visited the horse country and took a morning canter: "Queen Brings Reign to Kentucky." Headline writers live for heads like that one.

raise / raze

Bob Thomas, who writes about movies for The Associated Press, described a key scene in *Witness*, one of the best movies of 1985. The scene "depicts the razing of a barn in Pennsylvania Amish country."

In Salem, Va., the Times-Register carried a photo of a rubbled downtown lot. Said the caption: "Several houses have been raised along Clay Street near the corner of Broad and Main streets where a group of buildings are scheduled for demolition early next year."

Across the state, in Suffolk, the News-Herald carried an item of local business news. A real estate developer "must raise some existing structures in order to build new ones."

First you *raze*; then you *raise*. The verb *raze* goes back to the sixteenth century. It probably qualifies as an absolute word, not subject to modifiers of degree. A building might be partly demolished, or partly destroyed, but to *raze* is to level a structure altogether.

rampant / rampart

A book reviewer in the Asbury Park (N.J.) Press had kind words for *The House on Octavia Street* by Jacqueline La Tourrette. "This intriguing novel is set in turn-of-the-century San Francisco, when white slavery, murder and mayhem ran rampart and nobody did too much about it."

How's that again? Things can run *rampant*, meaning they can run wild, get extravagant, go crazy, but running *rampart* is tough because a *rampart* is a fortification. It's also a noun. For the record, in heraldry an animal standing on its hind legs and pawing the air is an animal *rampant*. Lions, mostly.

raptor/rapture

In Langley, Wash., the director of the South Whidbey Wildlife Center wrote to the letters column of the local Record. As it came out in print, the director explained that "what we release here on the Island is mainly rabbits, birds, redtailed hawks, raptures, eagles, lots of pigeons and doves . . ."

In Bend, Ore., a staff writer reported in the Bulletin about efforts to provide roosts for hawks and eagles. He quoted a wildlife biologist: "Rafters don't like to be around populated areas, so they won't roost on barns or farmhouses." The biologist said "the most abundant species of rafters in the Fort Rock area are bald and golden eagles, redtailed hawks and owls." The headline writer put a helpful streamer over the story. "Rafting Birds Receive New Home."

It's a fair guess that the copy editor in Langley and the news room in Bend had only a nodding acquaintance, if any acquaintance at all, with *raptors*. These are birds of prey—hawks, eagles, falcons, even condors. To observe raptorial birds may well be a source of rapture, for they are the kings and princes of the bird world, and no one who ever has seen a falconer at work is likely to forget the deadly beauty of the swordsmen of the sky.

reek/wreak

In the Idaho State Journal, a movie critic recalled some of the famous films of director Brian De Palma. *Carrie*, one of the best, "was the story of a girl who reeks havoc on her high school prom with telekinetic powers . . ."

In the real estate section of the Chicago Sun-Times, a feature writer pointed to the risks of investing in rental

property. A neighborhood might go down; utility costs
could go up. Furnaces fizzle, roofs leak, and boilers have to
be replaced. "These woes can reek havoc with the bottom
line of an owner's budget."

Alas, something smells. The writers didn't want *reek*;
they wanted *wreak*, which incidentally may be pronounced to rhyme with cheek or check as you please.
About the only thing you can do with this verb is to wreak
either havoc or vengeance. To *reek* is to give off an offensive odor. To say that a person "reeks charm" or "reeks
with personality" is to say something nasty.

respectably / respectfully / respectively

This is a troublemaker, as a sportswriter for the Pittsburgh
Post-Gazette discovered when he answered his own rhet-
orical question. What ever happened to Jose Arcia, Tommy
Dean, and Ed Spiezio? He first identified them: "They
were, respectably, the starting second baseman, shortstop,
and third baseman of the original San Diego Padres, circa
1969."

A wire service reporter had a different problem early in
1985 in quoting the executive director of a petroleum association: "Oil prices weakened in a year in which U.S. oil
demand increased rather respectfully."

The reporter presumably meant to say that demand had
increased *respectably*. The sportswriter truly may have
intended to say that the three infielders played a *respect-
able* brand of baseball—not anything brilliant, or outstand-
ing, just fairly good journeyman baseball—but the chances
are that he was trying to field the adverb *respectively*, i.e.,
in the order given, when it took a bad bounce and went
through his legs.

right / rite

At the Miami Herald, a music critic gave a rave review to
country singer Hank Williams, Jr. "After forty-nine albums

and countless years on the road, Williams is an artist in his own rite."

Across the country, at the Capitol Hill Times in Seattle, a news item reported an arrest: "The officer parked his car and approached the woman, advising her of her rites."

A *rite* is a ritual, for heaven's sake; it is a ceremonial act. If the officer was advising the woman of her rites, he must have been advising her about extreme unction. To be sure, the litany by which police read a suspect his Miranda rights is a kind of rite, but it's wrong to confuse the two.

role/roll

At the Danville (Va.) Community College, the Student Government Association published the minutes of its October meeting: "After the meeting was called to order, a role was passed around." This was perhaps because the acting president was presiding.

At the Trenton (N.J.) Times, a columnist analyzed the troubles of vice-presidential candidate Geraldine Ferraro: "Right now, Ferraro is attempting to have the best of two separate rolls." She had a Parker House in one hand and a hard roll in the other.

In This Week magazine, a movie columnist let us know that Clint Eastwood "is a fairly daring Hollywood star in terms of the rolls he plays." In La Gaceta, an otherwise unidentified publication, a columnist says that actor Beau Bridges, in a film about auto racing, "demonstrates what he can do with a challenging roll." Those hot-buttered things do have a way of dripping.

An actor's *roll* is either his tumble or his bread. The right word is *role*, an assumed part. At the community college they were passing around a different *roll*, a list of members who were present.

rout/route

In the News-Star-World of Monroe, La., a sportswriter picked Rayville to beat Farmerville by eight, even though "Farmerville looked good in a route of Bernice last week."

If Farmerville had handed Bernice a route, Farmerville would have been giving directions. The game was a *rout*, a disastrous and overwhelming defeat in an atmosphere of wild confusion. It's a word to be used with discriminating care. Only the most lopsided defeats are routs.

saddle/straddle

An outfit called HALT, which I take to be an acronym but know not what of, put out a flier on how its members could

make better use of legal services. The flier quoted the Federal Times on how HALT's manual on "shopping for a lawyer" could be of help: "It can save you money, time, and the headache of being straddled with a shyster."

Being straddled with a shyster would be a lamentable experience, sure enough. To straddle is to be sitting astride something—a fence, maybe, or an issue—but it's a most uncomfortable position. What the folks at HALT intended to warn against was being *saddled* with a shyster, i.e., to have the shyster on your back.

sea/see

These homophones are hard to mess up, but the respected Washington Post brought it off in a piece from Cairo about the Christian Coptic Church. The church now is headed by Pope Shenouda III, whose official title is "Pope of Alexandria and Patriarch of the Sea of St. Mark."

That's a sea that somehow does not appear on maps of the region. The bearded gentleman is patriarch of a *see*, a nice thirteenth-century word meaning the seat of ecclesiastical authority.

sedentary/sedimentary

It's funny how words come out the wrong way. In the TV column of the Kansas City Star, readers could learn something about John Hillerman, an actor who plays the role of Higgins on *Magnum, P.I.* It appears that "playing a reserved, sedimentary character really suits him."

Playing a sedimentary character would test the resources of any actor; he would have to build up the part layer by layer. The impeccable, immaculate, almost imperturbable Higgins is more or less a *sedentary* character, which is to say that he sits a good deal of the time.

sequenced/sequined

Curious things go through the absent-minded heads of people who edit copy. The AP reported from Pinedale, Wyo., on the town council's action in voting down a proposed ordinance to ban guns. "Before the council meeting, a woman in a sequenced dancing outfit and a person in a gorilla suit passed out balloons . . ."

I once interviewed a woman in a sequenced dancing outfit. She was a stripper by trade. Garment by garment, she went from a Southern belle in hoopskirts to a contemporary tigress in nothing at all. She was sequenced, all right, and everything came off bar by bra to a medley from *Showboat*.

The woman in Wyoming, to get back to linguistics, probably was in a *sequined* outfit. Some centuries ago sequins were small gold coins in the Near East; they're now the tiny metallic petals that adorn a dress.

setters/sitters

The ad in the Mobile Press-Register evoked a depressing image:

> CERAMIC tile sitters needed.
> Position Permanent.

It remains to be said only that a *setter* is not just an artisan who sets tile but also a bird dog that sits when the dog finds quail.

sew/sow

It is no use asking me why *sew* and *sow* should both be pronounced to rhyme with *hoe* and *slow*, because these things are stumpers. Neither do I understand why the *bow* of a ship rhymes with the *bough* of a tree, and the *bow* of an archer rhymes with the *toe* of a shoe. These things were put into English to irritate the French, whose superiority about their language can be infuriating.

In an editorial in The Miami Herald about mines in the Red Sea, we learn that U.S. forces "are helping to clear the seas of mines sewn by culprits yet unknown." In the Indianapolis Star, a columnist tells us the Democratic Party is failing to attract good candidates for the General Assembly: "The party is simply not sewing the seeds of future victories." In the Roanoke Times & World-News, the headline over an agronomy column informs us that "Lemon Balm Seeds Should be Sewn in Spring."

The culprits who wrote those sentences (*culprits* is a word, like *behooves*, much loved by editorial writers) didn't mean to stitch mines or to stitch seeds; they meant to *sow* them, to scatter them, to cast them broadly. Again, this is the *sow* that rhymes with *hoe* and not the *sow* that rhymes with *plough*. We will teach aliens a thing or two yet.

shear/sheer

In Lancaster, Pa., the coach of Lancaster's Catholic football team promised that if his team beat Conestoga Valley he would shave his head. Sure enough, the Catholic eleven triumphed. Punned the New Era: It was "shear delight." There wasn't anything delightful about an incident in Denver, when hundreds of honest-to-God working cowhands came to town for the annual Western Stock Show and Rodeo. Boys will be boys. The cowhands caught up with some long-haired hippies at Grant Street and East 17th Avenue and gave them some unrequested haircuts. The Denver Post explained that the haircuts were administered "with sheep sheers."

From Atlantic City, a reporter for The Associated Press undertook to describe the dress of Miss Massachusetts. "She wore a red-sequined sheath slit to the thigh and accented with feathers and shear sleeves."

Very well. The words do get confused. To *shear* something is to cut it off—hair, or wool, or hedges. When a pun is a *sheer* delight, the pun is an utter, unqualified, absolute delight. If your purpose as a writer is to put a sexy woman in a transparent and flimsy nightie, be sure it's *sheer* and not *shear*.

shoe-in / shoo-in

Why do reporters have such trouble with this one? It's curious, because there is no such word as *shoe-in*. Yet slip-ups happen all the time. In Florence, S.C., the Morning News carried an AP story about an election to the state Senate in which there was only one candidate running. Said the headline: "Shoe-in Fills Lancaster Senate Post." Across the continent, the Portland Oregonian noted that Ron McCarty had won the Democratic nomination for the Oregon House of Representatives. With no Republican in the field, "McCarty is a shoe-in for the post."

These candidates were *shoo-ins*. The verb and the interjection date from the fifteenth century. If we want to get chickens out of the yard or children out of the house, we cry "shoo!" The nuisances are *shooed* away, i.e., they are put to immediate flight. They scram. They disappear. There is no question about it. Thus a horse or a candidate who is a *shoo-in* is certain to run swiftly to victory.

Mencken touches upon *shoo-fly* in *The American Language*, but only as an ephemeral slang phrase that arose in the mid-nineteenth century and soon died out: "Shoo, fly, you bother me!" Why a rich Pennsylvania Dutch pastry should be known as a *shoofly pie* I cannot say, but I had a slice of one once in York, Pa., and it was fantastic.

sight / site

See the entry under *cite/sight/site*.

soluble/solvable

One of the problems with even the most sophisticated computers, reported The New York Times, is that the machines cannot recognize everyday objects and distinguish one from another. Inventors are hard at work in developing a synthesized sense of sight. "The result has been a burst of new ideas, techniques and ways of building computers that suggest the riddle may be soluble after all."

True enough, the lexicographers sanction the use of *soluble* in the sense of capable of being solved, so the Timesman's sentence is defensible. The trouble is that the first meaning of *soluble* is "susceptible of being dissolved." The writer could have avoided a flicker of misunderstanding by writing of a *solvable* riddle instead. A soluble riddle, at first glance, is a wet one.

spade/spayed

In the Bristol (Va.) Herald-Courier, the Humane Society asked for adoption of a two-year-old calico cat. "The cat has been spade," the paper said.

Nope. That cat had been *spayed*. The verb comes out of root words for sword; it means the surgical removal of ovaries from animals. The word has a precise clinical meaning, and ought to be used instead of "fixed" or "taken care of." Let us call a spade a spade.

stable/staple

In a feature story on Mexican food, the Fredericksburg (Va.) Free Lance-Star had a note on the jicama: "Pronounced 'hee-cah-mah,' this tuber is a stable in Mexico."

A former high-ranking Soviet official, now defected to the West, spoke at Ole Miss. The Oxford Eagle reported that the visitor said there is enough bread for everyone in Russia, "but rationing of stables such as meats is not uncommon."

To ration stables might involve putting two horses in one stall. The reporter wanted *staples*, i.e., commodities that are in constant use. The confusion is understandable. Certain elements in our diet are in fact *stable*; coffee, tea, eggs, flour, and sugar are used all the time. In Mexico the people may eat jicamas at breakfast, lunch, and dinner. Their place is fixed; it is stable. But the commodities themselves take the noun *staple*, leaving *stable* for an animal shelter.

stationary/stationery

A writer has to learn the difference, and if he can't remember the difference (a common failing), he will have to keep looking up the spelling. An AP correspondent in Mobile hadn't looked closely enough. A local librarian, after a visit to Russia, "appeared on television last Thursday and read a brief statement he had written on hotel stationary."

He wanted *stationery*. There's no such noun as *stationary*. We can have in meteorology a *stationary front*, one that is not moving, but if the reference is to writing paper it's *stationery*. For mnemonic help: Remember that there's an *er* in *paper*.

stile/style

The Chicago Tribune sent a transportation writer to interview Henry and Clara Davis, who run a concession stand at the 95th and State Street station of the El. It's the CTA's busiest station. "Nearly 7.1 million riders board through the turnstyles every year."

Those aren't turnstyles that chew up a fare card. They're *turnstiles*. These ingenious passageways date from the mid-seventeenth century; they are so designed that persons must go through them, on foot, one at a time. A turnstyle might be a changing hemline.

straight/strait

In naval parlance, a *strait* is a narrow passage connecting two large bodies of water. We have the Straits of Gibraltar, and ships go straight through them. By extension, we tend to think of a strait as anything binding or constricting, but the words get confused.

In the Spokane Chronicle, an official of Washington State University defended the university's sale of certain stadium tickets. The school needed the money, and "I assumed incorrectly that the students were concerned with our financial straights."

In the Patriot-News of Harrisburg, Pa., a headline told us that "A Less Straight-laced Times of London Loses Some Luster, But Gains Circulation."

The Roanoke Times & World-News editorialized about teen-aged pregnancies, and recalled the day when "nice girls" were ostracized if they got pregnant. That may have been unfair to those young women "who were penalized excessively for one or two departures from the strait and narrow."

The preferred usages are *straitjacket*, *straitlaced*, and *straight and narrow*. All straight?

taught/taut

A staff writer for The Seattle Times once tried to explain what was going on in a painting titled "Tight Dally, Loose Latigo," by Western artist Charles M. Russell. "That's the one in which a cowboy has tied his lariat too tightly on his saddlehorn, and the roped steer has pulled it taught under the horse's belly."

The mind wanders. Perhaps the steer had been to college, but it's a better bet that the writer wanted *taut* and forgot to rope it down.

tempera/tempura

The AP provided an obituary from Roswell, N.M., on artist Peter Hurd, who died at eighty in 1984. The writer quoted David Turner, director of the Fine Arts Museum in Santa Fe: "His work in egg tempura is some of the finest produced in this century."

The director didn't say *tempura*, which is a process of cooking. He said *tempera*, which is a process of painting. To cook shrimp tempura, for example, you dip a dozen sizable shrimp in a very light batter and fry them swiftly in deep fat. To paint with tempera, you use egg yolks instead of oil to mix with your dry pigment. To quote Cicero, you cry, O tempera! O mores!

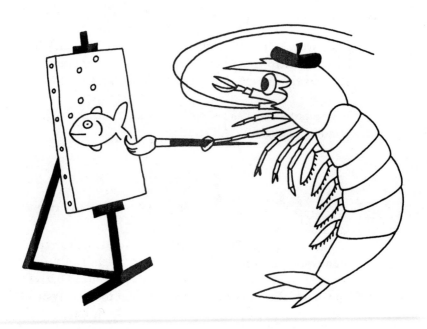

tenant/tenet

In The Miami Herald, a book reviewer reflected on the character and career of Harry S. Truman: "He lived the tenants of a non-theoretical but rigid American ideology."

In a government publication the author expounded "the tenants of a sound policy on public housing," which really messed things up.

In The Birmingham News, an editorial deemed it unfortunate that a post-election poll had found that a woman's presence on the Democratic ticket had proved a net liability. "To project stereotypical attributes to men or women is to reject the basic American tenant of judging the individual by his or her own merits."

In each instance the writers were talking about *tenets*, not *tenants*. Houses have tenants; they are the people who pay the rent. Creeds and philosophies and policies have tenets; they are the principles and doctrines of a movement. It is from these arguments and discussions that a familiar inquiry has arisen: Tenets, anyone?

tensile/tinsel

The Suttle Apparatus Corporation of Lawrenceville, Ill., sent a letter to distributors and customers promoting the merits of its products: "Our gold contact wires have as a minimum, 50 micro inches of gold plating over 100 micro inches of nickel over Grade A phosphor bronze wire having 150,000 lbs. of tinsel strength."

What kind of strength is that? Tinsel is that silver stuff you hang on Christmas trees. It's flimsy, it's cheap, it's gaudy. What the vice president for sales and marketing meant to brag about was the *tensile* strength, a measure of the stress the wire can bear without breaking.

threw / through

In Stuart, Fla., more than two hundred residents of Manatee Pocket petitioned the county attorney to draw up an ordinance restricting the time a boat can anchor without being moored to a dock. Nothing much happened. The Stuart News quoted the leader of the group: "Somehow our petition fell threw the bureaucratic cracks."

The staff writer stumbled over a preposition and got thrown for a loss. She wanted *through*, which Colonel McCormick insisted to the end of his days should be spelled *thru*.

throne/thrown

Thinking of getting thrown: A headline writer at the Kankakee (Ill.) Journal took a tumble on a story about a corn-growing contest. A Watseka farmer had won the first prize four times, but meager rainfall defeated him in 1983. "Drought Dethrowns the Corn King," read the head. The monarch who is overthrown is not dethrowned; he's *dethroned*. He hasn't a chair to sit in. This next observation has nothing to do with the homophone at hand, but a *throne* is the third order of angels, ranking just behind seraphim and cherubim and above such lesser orders as dominions, virtues, powers, and principalities. Try working this trivia into your next dinner table conversation and see what it gets you.

tic/tick

A reviewer for the Knight-Ridder papers didn't think much of a film called *The Warrior and the Sorceress*, in which David Carradine plays the role of a warrior. The hero wanders into a desert village in which two greedy factions are fighting over the town's only well. "One of the town's factions is governed by a big, fat guy with a facial tick who has a naked princess in chains in the basement."

A *tick* is a little bloodsucking insect that loves to feed on cows, dogs, and humans. If the thin guy really had a tick on his face, he should have dislodged it with a hot needle and then squashed the critter. The guy in the movie had a *tic*, a spasmodic, recurring twitching of a muscle in his face. Other *tics* are all around us. The TV sportscaster who keeps saying "of course" has a verbal tic; the songwriter who keeps rhyming *moon* and *June* has a prosodic tic. Such tics tick us off.

toe/tow

These mischievous fellows, *toe* and *tow*, have sent many a writer to the foot of the line.

The Scripps-Howard News Service had a piece about sports announcers Keith Jackson and Digger Phelps. It appeared that Phelps was moving up, but Jackson was having his troubles. "When ABC picked Al Michaels over Jackson for track, Jackson towed the company line. But, he didn't enjoy it."

In the Martin County (Fla.) News a movie reviewer summed up an episode in a forgettable film called *Grandview, U.S.A.* Two teen-agers park and neck after the senior prom, but when "the expensive Caddy sinks about four feet in the mud, the lovebirds become filthy and have to walk quite a way to get a toe truck."

The national Star serialized a book about the *real* Johnny Carson and his longtime sidekick Ed McMahon. At one point when their show was just catching on, Carson got it in his head that McMahon was trying to upstage him. Carson told him to cut it out. "If McMahon didn't tow the line, he'd find himself on the unemployment line."

The Smithfield (N.C.) Herald stubbed its toe also. In an editorial flaying Jesse Helms for painting Gov. Jim Hunt as a "Mondale liberal," the editor said that anyone who follows politics should know by now "that Jim Hunt and Walter Mondale, though both are Democrats, do not tow the same line on all the issues confronting voters."

Over the millennia, *toe the line* has left the running track and moved into general use. The phrase applies to almost any area of regimented conduct in which subordinates are expected to follow orders or policies without deviation. As for the muddy teen-agers, they were looking for a *tow* truck. The verb dates from before the twelfth century, and the noun—in the sense of "give us a tow"—from about 1600.

transgress/transpire

The Towanda (Pa.) School Board wasn't altogether pleased with football coach Jack Young, but after two fractious sessions and three close votes, the board agreed to renew his contract for another year. Reported the Daily Review: "After being informed of what transgressed, Young had no comment."

I take note of this confusion only because it provides a handy opportunity to speak to the matter of *transpire*. That was the verb the reporter was looking for. (To *transgress* is to violate some law or rule, to exceed a boundary or limit.) But the reporter should not have been looking for *transpire*. He should have been looking for *happened*, or *occurred*, or *took place*. To *transpire* means to become known. This particular school board met in executive sessions. It would have been correct to report that after the meetings "it transpired that the board had taken three close votes"; that is, after the meetings it became known that the board had taken the votes, and so on.

troop/troupe

The word for soldiers, Boy Scouts, itinerant apple pickers, and almost every other organized aggregation of humans having a common purpose is *troop*. The exception—an exception worth preserving—is a group of traveling actors. They constitute a *troupe*.

tudor/tutor

A classified ad in the Roanoke (Va.) Times at least had consistency in its favor:

TUDORING—vicinity of South Roanoke. English and related subjects. All ages.

Would anyone want to be tudored in French?

vain/vein

A television critic on the West Coast covered a press conference at which comedian Bill Cosby made some serious comments on his TV series. It is important, Cosby said, to show that if people really love their children, families are the same all over. "Cosby could have gone on in that vain," said the critic, "but it was nap time for the kids."

Cosby wasn't going on "in that vain." The wandering word was *vein*, as in a vein of coal. The errant *vain* comes from the Latin for *empty*, and can mean not only conceited but also idle, futile, useless, and foolish.

vice/vise

In West Palm Beach the Post carried a Page 1 streamer: "Schmidt Warns World Still in Economic Vice." In Hartford, the Courant had an intriguing headline over a story about a member of the State Board of Education who became innocently involved in a power struggle: "State Education Leader Caught in Political Vice." In Birmingham, the AP quoted a judge who was hearing the complaint of a company engaged in disposing of toxic wastes. The company had been hard hit by a ruling from a state agency. "The company was caught in a vice," said the AP. In Portland, Ore., Sears advertised a "3-position vice, was $29.99, now $15."

Come now! A world in an economic *vice* is a world with terrible imbalances in trade. Political *vice* is corruption. The Alabama company was being squeezed inexorably between two opposing forces. That is the function of a *vise.* The noun comes from the Latin *vitis,* vine, out of the screw that brings the jaws of a vise together. I did not know until I checked, but *vise* also is a transitive verb; you can *vise* a person or a thing. Remarkable.

waist / waste

The Savannah Morning News had something to say about the city's observance of St. Patrick's Day. Like Mardi Gras in New Orleans, the occasion is keyed to religious tradition but it abounds in what some might see as paganism. "For example, 86 of the 87 females who stripped to the waste on River Street last March 17 probably couldn't tell you the difference between a high mass at the Cathedral and a low tide on Chimney Creek."

The Roanoke Times & World-News painted a graphic picture of the rescue of campers whose campsite was swept away by a flood on the New River. "When rescue workers arrived, Simpson had climbed a tree and Vickers was standing in water up to his waste."

It was their *waists* the women of Savannah stripped to, and it was his waist that Vickers was standing in water up to. If those of you who have a thing about sentence-ending prepositions would prefer a recasting: It was his waist up to which Vickers in water was standing.

waive / waver

Sen. Edward M. Kennedy, D-Mass., sent a letter to elderly constituents who inquired about the rising costs of health care. Said the senator: "My commitment to Medicare recipients has never waivered."

In Harrisburg, Pa., police arrested a man on charges of impersonating an officer. The Evening News reported that the fellow had pushed a citizen against a car and asserted he was from the vice squad. "Then he waived something that resembled identification."

In Portland, a sportswriter for the Oregonian rued the way in which TV has taken over basketball. "As long as all those dollars are waived in front of the NCAA's nose, who is to resist?"

From the Environmental Defense Fund came a newsletter asserting, among other things, that "the American public has demonstrated unwaivering support for environmental legislation."

Wavered, senator! You never *wavered*! These confusions go back at least to the time in the early 1800s when a British warship halted an American schooner and took prisoners. In response to a violent U.S. protest, the word came back that Britannia not only rules the waves; she also waives the rules. In that sense, says Webster's, to waive is "to dismiss as if with a wave of the hand." In more familiar uses, to *waive* is to relinquish a right or at least to put off its enforcement. To *waver* is to hesitate, to falter, to go first one way and then another.

ware/wear

The Citibank folks sponsored an ad in Consumer Views to encourage safety in the home: "Never take the stairs in stockinged feet or slippery footware . . ." In Seattle, the Highline Times carried an ad for "comfortable nightware."

Comfortable nightware might be a fine thing for people with pots, but *nightwear* would be lots more comfortable.

way/weigh

There is such a thing as *under weigh*, but it's a phrase to forget unless you're writing for a naval publication. A ship that is *under weigh* has just hoisted its anchor or released its mooring lines; a moment later it is *under way* (two words), just as any venture or proceeding can be said to be *under way* once it gains momentum. There's also an adjective *underway* (all one word), but it too has a special mean-

ing in naval parlance: *underway replenishment,* and *underway refueling* are supply maneuvers at sea. Once a vessel (or a venture) is *under way,* it begins to make *headway* (one word) unless it runs into a *head wind* (two words). Almost all words carrying the prefix *head-* are spelled as one word. A curious exception is *headhunter* (one word), but *head-hunting* (hyphenated). The lexicographers may explain this. I can't even explain how I got into H words in the W section.

welt/whelp

The Mount Airy (N.C.) News had an item about a dairy farmer who shot at a pack of dogs harassing his herd. "He thought he might have hit one or two because some of the dogs whelped in pain."

Another Southern paper, not otherwise identified, described a woman who had been severely beaten by an assailant. She was "black and blue and had whelps all over."

If a bitch had a tough delivery, she might very well "whelp in pain," but those dogs weren't whelping; they were yelping. The victim of assault wasn't knee-deep in puppies; she suffered *welts*.

wench/winch

In Fort Collins, the Coloradoan sent a reporter to do a feature story on the Engineering Research Center at the Foothills Campus of Colorado State University. There the reporter found lab technician Rob Nelson. He was watching instruments "as a wench, exerting 10,000 pounds of pressure, pulled back on a debarked, 50-foot Douglas fir lying parallel to the floor." The idea of this stress test is for "a wench to bend the pole until it breaks."

A classified ad in the Goldsboro (N.C.) Argus set forth an offer no red-blooded mariner could resist:

> 250-LB boat wench, used but
> in good condition. $150.

250-LB BOAT WENCH, USED BUT
IN GOOD CONDITION.

Ah, those girls of the golden West! And, ah, those seagoing girls of the Carolina coast! A *winch*, which was the
mislaid word, is a machine for hoisting or hauling heavy
weights. A *wench* is a lusty young woman. Shakespeare, in
As You Like It, described Audrey as "a country wench."
She was an ill-favored thing, as Touchstone said, "but
mine own."

wet/whet

The Historical Society of Cocalico Valley, Pa., sent a letter
to prospective bidders at the society's annual auction in
May. Among the items to be sold were primitives, glass-
ware, china, rare books, and decorated brides' boxes "just
to wet your appetite." A lip-licking event, we assume.

The Wichita Falls Sunday Times toppled into the
opposite pitfall. "Rain Whets Parched North Texas," read
the streamer. Well, something in North Texas needed to be
sharpened, especially the attention of a headline writer.

while/wile

In Ohio, the Canton Repository had a spread of holiday
photos. Read a caption: "Some preferred the tranquility of
a late evening cruise at Nimisilla Reservoir to wile away
the Labor Day weekend."

In California, a reader wrote to the letters column of the
San Francisco Chronicle in order to fire a sarcastic shot at
Geraldine Ferraro for getting TV coverage of a grocery
shopping expedition with her husband. This is how "U.S.
congressfolk and apartment house landlords wile away
some weekend time."

In Georgia, a columnist for the Carrollton Times Geor-
gian spun a story about a drunk who walked through a
cemetery and fell into an open grave. Earlier in the day the
fellow had "wiled away the time over at a pub."

Both *while* and *wile* can mean "to pass time pleasurably," but *while* is the better word. For this reason: Whether as noun or verb, *while* has but one meaning; it always has to do with an interval of time. By contrast, *wile* has two meanings. As a noun, it conveys the idea of a trick or deception. In the verb form, a woman might wile away the afternoon at a beauty parlor; thus made more alluring, in the evening she might wile her man.

While we're on the general subject: You don't stay for awhile. You either stay awhile or you stay for a while.

who's/whose

The Washington Post ranks toward the top of anyone's list of the ten best newspapers in the land. Its reporters and editors are among the best paid in the press, but even the brightest heads may nod. "Who's Party is This?" asked a headline over an item about a political candidate who had discreetly failed to identify herself with any party. During the Democratic primaries of 1984, a correspondent quoted Joe Grandmaison "who's current candidate, Glenn, is waging a very un-McGovernite campaign."

Give the miscreants nine lashes with a wet noodle! *Who's* is a contraction of *who is*. *Whose* is the possessive adjective or pronoun: *whose* party; *whose* candidate.

yoke/yolk

The Youngstown Vindicator carried a photo spread of activewear (a word the lexicographers have not yet discovered) that had been created by designer Theoni V. Aldredge. Among the outfits was "a deep armhole vest with drop yolk mini skirt."

The Hillsboro (Ore.) Argus quoted Chris Christiansen on a modern reenactment of a pioneer trek: "I would say that was the only yolk of oxen that will ever make it across the United States in our time."

The model in that armhole vest hadn't dropped an egg;

the designer had dropped a *yoke*, a shaped piece at the top of a skirt or at the shoulder of a blouse. A *yoke* is also the wooden bar by which two draft animals are harnessed. At the Argus, the yoke was on the person who wrote the story.